Lives in Cricket: No

C000056511

William Clarke
The Old General

Peter Wynne-Thomas

First published in Great Britain by
Association of Cricket Statisticians and Historians
Cardiff CF11 9XR.
© ACS, 2014

British Library Cataloguing-in-Publication Data.
A catalogue record for this book is available from the British Library.

ISBN: 978-1-908165-50-3
Typeset and printed by The City Press Leeds Ltd

Contents

CRICKET
AT TRENT BRIDGE GROUND.

The Grand Match between Eleven of ENGLAND and Fourteen of NOTTINGHAM, for £200 a-side, Thursday, Sept. 4, 5, & 6, 1845.

PRINTED ON THE GROUND.

ENGLAND.	How out.	1st Ins.	How out.	2d Ins.
Royston	run out	0	c Oscroft b Clarke	10
Pilch	run out	25	c Oscroft b Buttery	25
Dorrington	c Gilbert b Redgate	3	b Redgate	13
Hillier	not out	1	not out	
Box	c Gilbert b Redgate	13	b Tinley	0
Hayward	c Clarke b Redgate	3	S. Parr b Redgate	2
Dean	b Clarke	6	c Brown b Clarke	6
O Picknell	st Brown b Clarke	13	st Brown b Buttery	0
Cornwall	b Redgate	2	c Redgate b Clarke	46
Sewell	b Clarke	0	c G. Parr b Redgate	0
Martingale	b Clarke	23	b Tinley	21
Wide Balls				2
Byes		6		5
No Balls				1
Total		95		125

NOTTINGHAM.	How out.	1st Ins.	How out.	2d Ins.
W. Clarke	c Martingale b Hillier	10	b Dean	1
Barker	c Martingale b Hillier	3	b Dean	9
John Oscroft	c Dorrington b Hillier	6	c Pilch b Hillier	28
J. Guy	b Hillier	3	not out	28
G. Butler	run out	20	c Dean b Hillier	3
C. Brown	run out	1	c Cornwall b Hillier	7
G. Parr	c Hillier b Picknell	5	run out	7
S. Parr	b Dean	11	not out	40
Gilbert	not out	5	b Dean	0
W. Musters, Esq.	b Dean	6		
Tinley	c Royston b Hillier	4		
S. Redgate	c Dean b Hillier	1		
J. Buttery	c Box b Hillier	4		
T. Heath	b Hillier	3		
Wide Balls		1		
Byes		5		9
No Balls				
Total		88		134

Admittance 6d. each.—Ordinary, 2s. 6d. each, at Two o'Clock.—Refreshments on the Ground.—A large Marquee for Ladies. Denison's Cricketer's Companion to be had on the Ground.—Stand for Carriages.—No Dogs admitted.   B. S. OLIVER, PRINTER.

Scorecard of the match England v Fourteen of Nottingham,
played in 1845 – possibly the genesis of the format for the All-England Eleven,
which Clarke began in the following summer.

Introduction

Since Waterloo only two men have single-handedly changed the face of the known cricket world. The more recent is Kerry Packer, to whom we owe the majority of the innovations made since he set up his World Series Cricket. His predecessor is William Clarke, the subject of this present biography.

Clarke's activities, as they will be described in the chapters which follow, have to be set against the wider background of change taking place in English society. The old 'aristocratic' England was gradually becoming a more commercial and capitalist country; the great Reform Act of 1832 and the Municipal Corporations Act of 1845 took powers away from the gentry and placed them in the hands of a more commercial-minded class. Clarke's own commercial creation, the All-England Eleven, temporarily at least, led the cricket world and eclipsed the exclusive clubs of the south as well as the various ephemeral sides, some based on counties, supported by the gentry.

The transformation of the British economy, as industry became more important and agriculture (and hence rural life) declined, meant that more and more people moved to the towns and cities, where their numbers started to contribute to attendances at mass spectator sports. Interest declined in traditional rural sports, some 'boisterous, drunken and licentious', mostly free to spectators and often taking place on the many public holidays. Encouraged by churches and by secular groups, more respectable, 'rational' sports, the principal one in the 1830-1850 period being cricket, grew in popularity. Attendances grew, with many of the new, paying spectators coming from the skilled working and middle classes, after the income of those groups rose in real terms from 1822 onwards.

Some publicans, like Clarke, turned away from supporting the traditional ways and readily shifted to newer forms of entertainment. The railways, important for distributing goods and coal, started to carry participants and spectators to both the new and old cricketing venues. Rowland Hill's Penny Post made it easier for entrepreneurs to set up new events and fixtures and loosened reliance on the traditional holiday entertainments.

In so far as Clarke is remembered today, it is as founder of the Trent Bridge Cricket Ground, but its survival, when all the other pre-1850 northern 'professional' cricket grounds have faded away, is more due to the freehold owners, the Musters family, than any desire or influence on Clarke's part.

Clarke quit Trent Bridge and Nottingham in the spring of 1846 for a probable combination of reasons: his marriage broke down; seemingly there was little financial return from Trent Bridge as a sports ground, which at the time was well outside the town of Nottingham; and third, possibly he had already conceived his plan to create the All-England Eleven. I have been unable to ascertain which of these three reasons was the uppermost cause of his departure. However departure it was, for, despite taking part in well over 150 matches between September 1845 and September 1852, Clarke did not play at Trent Bridge in almost seven years.

Virtually from its creation in 1787, Lord's became the centre of the cricket elite, so much so that the most distinguished players, after the demise of the Hambledon Club, rarely desported themselves away from the south-east of England and some hardly stirred from Lord's itself. The major fixtures, Gentlemen v Players, Oxford v Cambridge and Eton v Harrow, brought together the cricketing greats and, aside from the notable amateurs – drawn of course exclusively from the gentry – who then became members of the very exclusive Marylebone Club, many of the best professionals sought engagements at Lord's in order to ensure a regular, if not substantial, summer income. A more detailed account of how Lord's came to dominate cricket is given in Chapter Seven.

In a single blow Clarke changed that cosy arrangement. He signed up (as Packer did one hundred and thirty years later) many of the outstanding performers of the 1840s – the names and abilities of his cricketers will be found in the body of this work. His idea of taking his team of stars throughout the United Kingdom, using the rapidly expanding railway network, rather bemused the pundits at Lord's, but Clarke proved them wrong. The general population flocked to watch Clarke's cricketers, who were widely recognised to include the best of the time, and the general standard of local players rose because they learned from playing against the leading practitioners.

That Clarke himself was the most effective slow bowler of his time as well as the most admired cricket tactician no doubt helped his pioneering enterprise. The esteem in which he was held by his contemporaries was emphasized when his portrait featured in the first edition of *The Cricket Field* – the only such portrait in the book. The writings of Bolland and Nicholas Felix underline still further Clarke's stature among cricket's intelligentsia. W.G.Grace's memoirs plainly demonstrate the tremendous influence that Clarke and the All-England Eleven had on cricket away from the metropolis and its environs – there can hardly be greater praise than that.

I have reproduced in full the 1852 vicious attack on Clarke, and Clarke's response – both have been alluded to previously, but as far as I am aware, the pieces have not hitherto been reprinted in any detail. In Appendix Two, I have reproduced Clarke's treatise *Practical Hints On Cricket* which first appeared in William Bolland's *Cricket Notes*: they really are worth reading through!

Clarke's fantastic success naturally bred jealousy and after 1852 perhaps he developed a dictatorial streak, which led to certain players, long after Clarke's death, telling derogatory stories about him – but similar comments emerged regarding W.G.Grace during the 1920s and 1930s. That's life.

Although the control of English cricket, on paper, reverted to the MCC and Lord's when Clarke's hand disappeared, he left the scene with cricket's profile enhanced to the extent that it was the most popular ball game in the British Isles, to play, watch and read about. With such teams as the United South of England and the Australians (every second summer, 1878 to 1890) following in his footsteps, or, more accurately, his train journeys, the enthusiasm felt for the sport by the man in the street continued to rise until the twentieth century, when football slowly but surely stole the limelight. Clarke was the man who created the 'modern' cricket scene, which is now just a memory in the minds of old men.

I hope that this, the first attempt to tell the story of Clarke's life, will make readers aware of the pivotal role Clarke played in our national pastime.

Chapter One
Tracing Clarke's Early Life

The usual opening for a biography is a setting of the scene when the subject is born – the circumstances of his parents and their immediate families, and how they came to be in the town or village at the time of their child's birth. At first glance this initial task for a William Clarke biography does not appear too arduous. J.F.Sutton's book, *Nottingham Cricket Matches from 1771 to 1853*, published in 1853, when William Clarke was in his pomp, contains a final chapter, *Sketches of Players*. William Clark's [sic] entry begins:

> ... the celebrated slow bowler, deservedly requires priority of notice. He was born in Nottingham, December 24, 1798 and (though yet stout and hearty) is consequently bordering on 'the sear and yellow leaf of life.' Many, however, may his years yet be! His father was a bricklayer, residing on Bunker's Hill, and Clarke was brought up to the same business ...

The baptismal register of St Mary's Church, a short walk from Bunker's Hill, contains an entry on 30 December 1798: 'William, son of John Clarke and Mary.'

Thus far the search for William and his parents has followed a predictable path. The next step in discovering more about John and Mary Clarke is the church marriage registers. A check through St Mary's registers from 1760 to 1798 produces:

3 September 1780	John Clarke and Mary Parrott
9 June 1783	John Clarke and Mary Ford
2 April 1786	John Clarke and Mary Richmond
1 July 1792	John Clark and Mary Bannister

An immediate reaction to this list is to eliminate the fourth entry because the surname is Clark and William's baptism gives Clarke as the father's surname. However the extant trade directories for the period rather contradict this assumption:

1799 and 1814	Clark, John, Bricklayer, Parliament Street
1818	Clark, John, Builder, Parliament Street
1825	Clark, John, Bricklayer, Parliament Street

Bunker's Hill was an off-shoot of Parliament Street and disappeared when the Victoria railway station and line was being constructed through the middle of Nottingham in the 1890s. The four trade directory entries coincide with the information Clarke gave to Sutton and thus the idea of eliminating the 1792 married couple would seem to be incorrect. The matter is slightly more confused by an inspection of the St Peter's Church marriage register, which contains a single John Clark(e) entry in the period searched:

20 January 1785   John Clarke (of East Leak [sic]) and Mary Bamford of this parish

St Peter's Church is marginally closer to Bunker's Hill than is St Mary's.

With the baptism registers of the period so sparing with their detail, I feel that John Clark and Mary Bannister are, based on the trade directories, the most likely parents, but even so it is impossible to extend the family of William Clarke beyond his two parents because there is no way of telling which children were born to which of the five sets of John and Mary Clark(e)s resident in Nottingham. The first census which provided researchers with such detail was not undertaken until 1841, so there are no alternative sources to the baptismal registers prior to the earliest detailed census.

Over recent years a number of members of the Clark(e) clan have contacted Nottinghamshire County Cricket Club claiming that they are related to William Clarke, but none has produced any convincing evidence. The most positive claim came from the descendants of William Clarke (1846-1902) and his brother Samuel (b 1829) from Old Basford. The former played occasionally for Nottinghamshire from 1874 to 1876. They claim that William Clarke was their uncle, but through family 'tradition'.

A.W.Shelton, a long-standing member of Nottinghamshire County Cricket Club's Committee and keen historian, spent both time and money in the months prior to the 1938 centenary of the Trent Bridge Ground researching the Clarke family, and more recently these researches have been extended by John Goulder and David Gretton, but with no breakthroughs regarding the famous cricketer's immediate ancestors.

Turning from the Clarke family itself to the town in which young Clarke spent his childhood and youth, it was a place of considerable turmoil, not to say misery. The population increased on average by 500 a year between 1801 and 1851, to a total of 25,000, yet the space in which the citizens lived remained unaltered; houses were crammed between houses and behind houses, hundreds of back-to-back dwellings were erected and people were sandwiched more tightly into the older properties. Due to the Inclosure Acts little or no building was allowed outside the confines of the town walls. Not until the second half of the nineteenth century was building permitted in the immediate countryside to the north and south of the town. For example, the Meadows area, which ran south towards the River Trent, was built on; to the north the Hyson Green development took place. The latter resulted in the 77 acres of The Forest Racecourse/cricket ground being encircled by bricks and mortar: the cricket ground was the venue for most of the major matches played by the Nottingham Club since records began in 1771. When Clarke first played on The Forest ground, he walked half a mile through fields before he reached the ground itself.

Nottingham was a town expanded during the first sixty years of the eighteenth century by its manufacturing of lace and hosiery through the use of framework knitting machines. However, at the time of Clarke's birth the Napoleonic Wars had cut off the lucrative continental market for goods produced in Nottingham. As a result the wages of the knitters sank

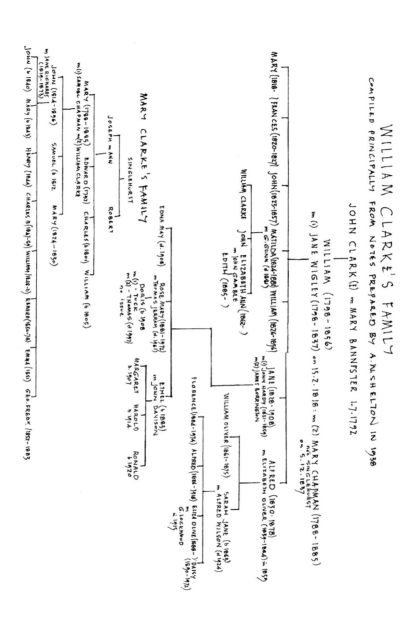

*The Clarke clan, compiled largely from the researches of A.W.Shelton.
It is, of course, none too easy to produce definitive versions of trees
where families have common names and variable spellings.*

from 12 shillings a week to a starvation eight shillings, a situation which led to the infamous Luddite Riots beginning in 1811/12, when handloom weavers smashed up the more advanced and productive knitting machines. Nottingham was definitely not a happy place in which to be growing up. Like the rest of Britain the increasing price of wheat made a difficult situation even more fraught.

William Clarke, according to his own account, left school to work with his father in the building industry, principally as a bricklayer; there appears to be no record of which school he attended though his subsequent life clearly indicates he was literate. Bricklaying itself is, of course, a skill requiring arithmetical capabilities. As a young adult he was 5ft 9in, so quite tall for his generation, and relatively slim, though by 1850 he had filled out to become 13st 11lb.

He was married on 15 February 1818 in St Nicholas Church, Nottingham to Jane Wigley – Clarke was described as from the parish of St Mary, whilst Jane was of St Nicholas. The two witnesses were John Lister Sharp and Catherine Wigley. On 29 December 1819 Clarke, having just reached the age of 21, was admitted as a burgess of Nottingham, when he is described as an innkeeper. The first child (a daughter, Frances) of William and Jane Clarke was baptised on 3 August 1820 at St Nicholas's Church, Clarke now being described as a victualler of Angel Row. Angel Row is a range of buildings leading out of Nottingham Market Square. The only inn contained there is The Bell, presently reputed to be the oldest in Nottingham, though two other inns dispute this claim. On the wall of the main bar of the inn is a time-line listing the landlords going back to the mid-eighteenth century. William Clarke is given as landlord from 1820. Immediately prior to him, and beginning in 1812 is Katharine Wigley. As a witness to Clarke's marriage was Catherine Wigley, it would be not too rash to assume that Catherine/Katharine Wigley was the mother of Jane Wigley. If the age at death of Jane Wigley, as given in the Nottingham newspaper in her obituary notice is correct, Jane was, like William, aged 19 at the time of her marriage.

A search through late eighteenth-century Nottinghamshire records

| WHEN BAPTIZED. | CHILD'S CHRISTIAN NAME. | PARENTS' NAME. | | ABODE. | QUALITY, TRADE OR PROFESSION. | BY WHOM THE CEREMONY WAS PERFORMED. |
		CHRISTIAN.	SURNAME.			
Nov. 2nd No. 698	Mary	William + Jane	Clark	Angel Row	Victualler	C Wylde

BAPTISMS SOLEMNIZED IN THE PARISH OF ST. NICHOLAS, IN THE TOWN OF NOTTINGHAM, IN THE YEAR 1818

The baptism certificate of William Clarke's oldest daughter, Mary. In 1818, state registration of births was still almost twenty years away.

indicates that there were two married couples both called William and Katharine Wigley. One couple resided for some time in Lenton, but that Katharine Wigley died the year before William Clarke married Jane Wigley so she could not therefore have been a witness at the marriage. There seems to be no extant record of either pair of William and Katharine Wigley themselves being married in Nottinghamshire, nor can be found a burial for the second Katharine/Catherine Wigley. At the time of writing, therefore, I have to accept that no definite details of William Clarke's wife's immediate ancestors beyond the assumption that William and Katharine/Catherine Wigley are probably her parents have been unearthed – hopefully some future historian will fill this gap.

The present frontage of the Bell Inn is little changed from the nineteenth century. Nicholas Pevsner, in his architectural survey of Nottinghamshire, dated the frontage circa 1830, although the English Heritage listings suggests circa 1820. If Pevsner is correct then it would appear that William Clarke was responsible for the façade we see today.

What is known, though, about Clarke's early cricketing? The answer is 'exceedingly little'. The game itself in Nottingham had been, like most other leisure activities, seriously affected by the political and financial climate caused by the long war with France. The Nottingham Club played three matches in 1800, a single one in 1801, then not a single fixture was recorded in the subsequent eleven years.

On 17 September 1813, the *Nottingham Review* printed the following piece:

> The manly and athletic game of cricket for which *the boys of Sherwood* have been so long and so justly famed, it was thought had fallen into disuse, if not disgrace, the match however, which was played in Gallows Close last Monday between eleven players of the town and eleven of the county, has removed all apprehensions of this nature.

Two matches were played, but no one surnamed Clark(e) featured in either eleven. The reason for these two trial matches was that Nottingham had challenged Leicester, giving Leicester the advantage of twenty-two players against the Nottingham twelve. The game was played on a neutral ground at Loughborough and the Nottingham Club was much too ambitious, losing by an innings. The losing twelve comprised six from the county side and six from the town. While this match was in progress Nottingham Second Eleven played Wollaton on Gallows Close: no Clarke features in this lesser match – he would now be aged 14. Sutton's book prints the score of the Loughborough game, but the author fails to mention it in his narrative history.

The *Nottingham Review* printed numerous local match details during 1814: in one, played at Holme Lane on July 19, two players, William Clarke and Wm Clarke, appeared for Cropwell Bishop v Radcliffe. It is impossible to say whether either of them is the cricketer of later fame. A William Clarke appears in matches for Cropwell each season from 1819 to 1822, so it seems probable this was another William Clarke.

The Bell Inn, Angel Row, Nottingham, where William Clarke was landlord from 1820 to 1837. A timber-framed building dating back to the fifteenth century, it was re-fronted in his time there. It was listed Grade II in 1982.

On 15 and 16 July 1816 Nottingham opposed Ripon at York Racecourse for 300 guineas a side and W.Clark appears in the Nottingham twelve – the biographical piece in Sutton's book notes that 1816 was 'the date of his first public match and he was held as a bowler of great reputation'. However, he is not credited with any wickets in the game and failed to score in his only innings. The scores of the local matches in which he must have played prior to being picked for the representative Nottingham team have been lost, so there is no way of being able to judge whether he was chosen for his batting or his bowling skills – Sutton rather jumps the gun with his comment regarding Clarke's bowling ability so early in his cricketing career.

From his subsequent life and his taking over of the Bell Inn, Clarke was a man set on personal financial advancement. It is worth noting the following passage from G.M.Crauford's *Sporting Life* series of articles featuring Nottinghamshire cricket, as this makes clear on the financial possibilities, good or bad, for Nottingham players at the time of Clarke's debut. Crauford's interview involves the Nottingham v Barrow and Mountsorrel match played in October 1815. The narrator is Joe Dennis, a Nottingham publican and captain of the Nottingham side.

I had invested rather largely on that match, and but for an unexpected slice of luck, should have lost at least £120; *imprimis,* I had laid one bet of 50 guineas that Nottingham won the game: secondly I had backed my runs in my two innings to be half as many as those made by our opponents in the first innings, and besides these large stakes, I had minor bets, varying from a sovereign to a 'fiver' on the result and on various points of the contest.

Now, you are aware that the Sixteen got 48 runs in the first innings to our 50 – anybody's match, so far; but I only made 6 runs in my first, and had consequently 18 to make in my second innings to land my second bet. The Sixteen finished their second innings for 73, thus setting Notts 72 to win, and the odds were decidedly against us, when at five o'clock I sent in Humphrey Hopkin and E.Pacey, with strict instructions to keep up their wickets, if possible, till time should be called, and not to care about getting runs, as we could do better next morning when fresh and in a clearer light, and without the long shadows.

To my horror, after Pacey had made two runs off the first ball, he was stumped off the next. I next sent in Richard Warsop, the only man on whom I could depend, telling him to be sure and save his wicket.

Soon, however, I had the mortification of seeing him bowled without a run. I was now in a towering passion; my £120 seemed hopelessly lost; and I knew that if the game was to be won I must do it myself. I had lent my favourite bat to Warsop, so I went to meet him; well, when he gives me the bat, he says (you know his way of sometimes shutting one eye when he speaks to you), 'Joe, what a fool I was to let that there ball knock my wicket down.'

I really felt in such a rage that I yelled out, "Get out of my way, or I'll knock out your brains with the bat", in fact I was so excited that I felt more like a madman than a rational being.

My first ball was extremely enticing, and, being very eager to hit, I stepped in too far, and, not getting properly hold of the ball, it touched just below the bat handle, and spinning in the air, fell into Shadrach Hunt's hands, but, oh what a release when I saw it slip through his fingers, hit his breast, and roll on to the ground!

From that moment I felt that the game was ours. I called for a glass of brandy, threw up my hat, and kicked it away, and shouted out, 'Now, Humphrey, do you keep your wicket up, and I'll whop 'em,' for I felt invincible.

That evening we got 45 runs, and carried out our bats, and the next morning Nottingham won by four wickets, but I shall always believe that if Shadrach Hunt had caught that first ball, the remaining eight men (including Tom Warsop, Leeson, Jefferies and Peter Bramley) would not have got 20 runs and that in point of fact that ball decided the match!

According to the *Nottingham Review* the match was for 80 guineas a side. It was played at Bunny, a large village a few miles south of Nottingham, and lasted four days. Further insight into how the Nottingham Club operated financially is revealed in 1818 when Nottingham played England, when Clarke was a member of the Nottingham team, but is again not credited with a wicket. The match was arranged for £150 a side, in addition to which Nottingham agreed to pay £40 towards the expenses of bringing the England team from London. The organizers of the match were Joe Dennis for Nottingham, and George Osbaldeston Esq for England. The latter was putting up the entire stake money for England. He failed to come to Nottingham as he was with a shooting party in Scotland. The England players could not raise their £75, but agreed on £25 a side. After the match began the England players announced that they could not really even afford the £25 and wished to play purely for honour. This caused problems because the Nottingham stake had been collected from numerous cricket supporters, some individuals giving as little as 3s 6d towards the total. The Nottingham Club felt that the England party had been 'extremely ill-used by their match-maker' and gave the England players £30 to pay for their return journey to London.

Of course Osbaldeston's absence could have had something to do with the same fixture the previous season. This match gained notoriety when William Lambert was accused by the Lord's authorities of selling the game and was thereafter never selected for a match on the Marylebone ground. Nottingham won by 30 runs. It was Clarke's second match for Nottingham and he scored just a single in his two innings. When interviewed later in life, Clarke maintained that Lambert had been unjustly accused of deliberately performing poorly in order to lose the game. The *Nottingham Review* after its report and detailed scores of the match continues with:

At the conclusion of the first match a second was made for 50 guineas, but on Thursday morning (when the parties appeared on the ground) a discovery being made that some very ungentlemanly proceedings had taken place, the Nottingham Club absolutely declined to play. Notwithstanding that, a number of both parties amused themselves till evening with their favourite exercise.

Nottingham scored 91 for the loss of 16 wickets; Clarke opened the batting and scored three; England did not have an innings. During these early years of his career in major matches, Clarke frequently went at the top of the order. Perhaps the loss of his eye affected his batting ability in later years.

One of the major difficulties in staging matches involving 'professional' players on the Racecourse in Nottingham and indeed, at the time in many other places, was that the spectators were not charged admission. Enclosed grounds for which an admission charge could be made were few and far between over the whole of England. This forced players to bet on the various aspects of each game, as well as the final result, in order to earn money. Cricket teams in the south of England were often picked and paid by rich benefactors, or speculators, but the Nottingham and Sheffield sides had to stand alone and gather money where they could.

Chapter Two

Clarke as a Bowler

Although it was not until five years after his initial 1816 Nottingham match that Clarke is credited with capturing any wickets for the team, two years earlier he and Humphry Hopkin are reported to have opposed Simpson and Terry in a single-wicket match on The Forest. Simpson and Terry won with ease, but one must assume that Clarke fancied his bowling skills, for in single-wicket a player needed to be an all-rounder. There is no written evidence of his bowling style until the famous 1826 match v Sheffield and Leicester, when the *Sheffield Independent* notes: 'Clark persevered in his old style of bowling, well pitched, but evidently too slow for the sharp-sighted Sheffielders.' It is interesting that the reporter uses the term 'old style of bowling'. We cannot tell whether this indicates that most bowlers were already employing round-arm and Clarke was continuing with under-arm, or whether Clarke was bowling slow, when most other bowlers bowled fast under-arm. Later commentators have stated that Clarke's success in the 1840s and 1850s as a bowler was due to the fact that he was almost alone then as an under-arm bowler, nearly everyone by that time having adopted the round-arm style. The match of 1826 between Nottingham and the combined forces of Sheffield and Leicester is considered by the ACS as the first first-class match played by Nottingham. Nottingham had beaten both Sheffield and Leicester individually and clearly the standard of Nottingham cricket had risen to the point that the club felt capable of opposing the combined opposition, hence the decision to judge the match 'first-class' – a more detailed discussion on first-class status of matches played in the early nineteenth century can be found in the relevant ACS guide to important matches.

With regard to the changing style of bowling during the same period, it is necessary to return briefly to the eighteenth century.

The first extant set of regulations is that set out by the Duke of Richmond and Alan Brodrick for the matches between their two teams in 1727. There is no clause in those regulations specifying how bowlers should deliver the ball. The earliest extant set of 'official' Laws are printed round the border of a handkerchief, referred to as the Humphry handkerchief, in R.S.Rait Kerr's splendid book *The Laws of Cricket: Their History and Growth* published by Longmans in 1950. Its date is unknown but might be about 1740. The date is not that important because when the Laws were first published in booklet form (in 1755) the details are the same except that the language is modernized. I am here quoting that 1755 booklet:

The bowler must deliver the ball with one foot behind the crease, even with the wicket; and when he has bowled one ball, or more, shall bowl to the number of four before he changes wickets, and he shall change but once in the same innings. He may order the player that is in at his wicket to stand on which side of it he pleases, at a reasonable distance. If he delivers the ball with his hinder-foot over the bowling crease the umpire shall call no ball, though it be struck or the player be bowled out; which he shall do without being asked and no person shall have any right to question him.

(I have set out this paragraph in full in order to emphasise the absence of any directive regarding the height of the bowling arm.)

Pycroft quotes Beldham as saying: 'When I was a boy say 1780 nearly all bowling was fast and all along the ground.' Beldham goes on to state that 'The art of bowling over the bat by *length balls* originated with the famous David [Harris].' Pycroft however qualifies this remark by saying that length bowling was introduced in David Harris's time, and by him first brought to perfection.

Nyren describes Harris's delivery:

> He would bring the ball from under his arm by a twist and nearly as high as his armpit, and with this action push it, as it were, from him. How it was the balls acquired the velocity they did by this mode of delivery, I never could comprehend ... in the prime of his playing he very rarely gave a toss, although the balls were pitched a full length. In bowling he never stooped in the least in his delivery, but kept himself upright all the time. His balls were very little beholden to the ground when pitched; it was but a touch and up again, and woe be to the man who did not get in to block them, for they had such a peculiar curve that they would ground his fingers against the bat ... He was considerably faster than Lambert, and so superior in style and finish that I can draw no comparision between them.

Harris first appears in matches printed in Haygarth's *Scores and Biographies* in 1782, though Nyren states Harris began playing in matches arranged by the Hambledon Club in 1778. He died in 1803 aged 48.

Nyren, in his notes on the Hambledon players, includes the following passage dealing with Tom Walker:

> About a couple of years after Walker had been with us, he began the system of throwing instead of bowling, now [*i.e.* 1833] so much the fashion. At that time it was esteemed foul play, and so it was decided by a council of the Hambledon Club, which was called for the purpose.

Thomas Walker was born in 1762 and his first match for Hampshire (or the Hambledon Club) given in *Scores and Biographies* is in 1786. If Nyren's comment is correct then 1788 would be about the year when the Hambledon Club ruled round-arm bowling illegal, but no such edict appears in the Laws of that date – indeed J.Wallis' broadsheet of the Laws printed on 25 May 1809 still contains the precise wording for bowlers as given in 1755.

By 1809, according to Pycroft, John Willes had been bowling round-arm for seven years. Nyren mentions Willes in his notes on Andrew Freemantle:

Upon one occasion when I had come up to London, I heard of a match being played in Lord's Ground, and of course made one of the spectators of my beloved amusement. Andrew Freemantle was in, and one of the new-fashioned bowlers, commonly called throwers, was bowling to him. His name was Wells [actually Willes], and I believe he came out of Sussex. He was the first I had seen of the new school, after the Walkers had attempted to introduce the system in the Hambledon Club.

No date is given for this match, but Freemantle's last major game was in 1810.

It was in the published Laws of 1811 that the ruling on the style of legal bowling first appears: 'The ball is to be bowled under-hand and delivered with the hand below the elbow.' However, several years later, when players clearly ignored this Law, a revised, more complicated version was issued (probably in 1816):

The ball must be delivered underhanded, not thrown or jerked, with the hand below the elbow at the time of delivering the ball. If the arm is extended straight from the body, or the back part of the hand be uppermost when the ball is delivered, or the hand horizontally extended, the umpire shall call *No Ball*.

Rait Kerr attributes this new law to William Ward and states that it is an example of how not to frame a law. Rait Kerr continues:

This enactment was a tactical blunder which was soon to cause trouble; the difficulty over the earlier law was not due to its wording, but to the weakness of the captains in allowing, and of the umpires in not stopping, illegal practices, which to-day [1947] would be dealt with by a MCC instruction to players and umpires.

As a result players continued to flout the law. Such flouting is succinctly described in Lord Harris's *The History of Kent County Cricket* under the biography of John Willes, where a sentence reads: 'When he (Willes) played on the side of Lord Frederick Beauclerk his bowling was fair: when against him the contrary.' Willes finally snapped during the match between MCC and Kent at Lord's in July 1822 – Lord Frederick was playing for MCC, Willes for Kent. Willes was no-balled when bowling early in the match and stormed off the ground. He played little cricket after that game.

John Willes played as an amateur for Kent. After he had retired another Kent amateur, G.T.Knight, took up the round-arm cause. The detailed correspondence which was published in the *Sporting Magazine* is reprinted in Denison's *Sketches of the Players*. Denison also gives the following preface to the details of three games played in 1827 and this preface explains the situation:

For the last three years there has not been so great an interest excited with the lovers of this manly game, as within this month (June 1827), on account of the grand match which has lately been made between All England and the County of Sussex, for 1,000 guineas a side, to be decided by three trials. The two first have been played, and both ended in favour of the County – at Sheffield by 7 wickets, and at Lord's by 3.

On the part of England there are one or two men from the neighbourhood of Sheffield, who have displayed great skill, and convinced the cricket world that the South must not, as heretofore, presume to wear the wreath for ever. On the part of Sussex there are some very fine players; but their victories have been, undoubtedly owing to a singular, novel, and perhaps we may say, unfair manner of bowling, by the over-cast from the arm, instead of the under-hand and graceful mode of the Old School. There has been considerable discussion on this point, – whether it could be allowed, and whether it shall be continued to be practised. The writer of this, an old cricketer, really shakes with fear of its adoption, as it certainly gives birth to the hope of gaining a wicket by chance, by a wild twist, instead of the fine steady length, as shown us in former times by Lumpy, Harris, John Wells, &c. It is true, these men could twist, but there was not that space taken by chance, as at present. The general complaint of the hitting now being so much superior to the bowling, can alone justify the experiment; and it is on that account it has been brought forward.

England beat Sussex in the third game, at Brighton on 23, 24 and 25 July 1827, by 24 runs. Two Sussex bowlers delivered the ball in round-arm style in all three matches; G.T.Knight bowled round-arm for England in the second and third matches.

The impossibility of operating the Law as amended in or about 1816 led to it being changed in May 1828 to: 'The ball shall be bowled. If it be thrown or jerked, or if any part of the hand or arm be above the elbow at the time of delivery, the umpire shall call 'No Ball'.' This simplified adjustment had little effect on the march towards round-arm bowling, but it was not until May 1835 that round-arm bowling was legalized by MCC: 'The ball must be bowled. If it is thrown or jerked or if the hand be above the shoulder in the delivery, the umpire must call 'No ball'.'

It is, however, ironic to read that William Lillywhite was frequently raising his arm above his shoulder by 1835 and other bowlers copied his lead. One player above all others captured the public's imagination as an all-rounder, Alfred Mynn. He made his debut in the Gentlemen v Players match at Lord's in 1832 and judging by the number of wides given it is obvious that he, and presumably G.T.Knight, bowled round-arm. In the following two seasons Mynn built up a great reputation as a hard-hitting batsman and a very fast round-arm bowler – every aspiring cricketer must have wished he could emulate Mynn, so he as much as anyone forced the change in the law noted in the previous paragraph. In fact the whole palaver occurred anew as the round-armers soon began to raise their arms above their shoulders, until the authorities again conceded defeat and over-arm was legalized in 1864, but that is long after Clarke's death and not a subject to be discussed here.

Although Clarke was to become a great innovator in the development of the game, first in Nottingham, then in the rest of the British Isles, yet curiously he remained wedded to a bowling style which was on its way out when he was still a youth. It's a conundrum. Spin bowling, whether over-arm or under-arm, demands exceptional skill and guile, often allied to years of practice, if a player is going to be effective at the highest level. According to some contemporary comments Clarke's bowling was not his main asset until he was in his thirties.

Undoubtedly he had great ability purely through the way he could vary the pace of his delivery without a noticeable change of action: linked to this was his accuracy of length and direction. Clarke's success was however also attributed to his careful study of the batting ability of his opponents. A number of players have commented on Clarke's habit of walking round the ground before the start of play and watching the home batsmen practising. One of the many examples will serve to illustrate this. The All-England Eleven were playing St Helens in a match in early May 1853. Joseph McCormick, then 18, was in the local side; he would captain Cambridge University three years later. He told A.W.Pullin of his first encounter with Clarke:

> I was practising when Clarke came walking round the ground with the ball in his hand. After watching me for a little while, he said, 'May I bowl you a ball or two?' Of course I was delighted at the favour. But, alas! I did not know his object was to demonstrate my own weakness. What happened? Old Clarke had evidently noticed that I was no slogger, but hit hard and low. The first ball he pitched to me well up, and I drove it for two. He then brought in George Anderson to twenty yards behind him, and bowled a similar ball and I hit it hard and straight into the Yorkshireman's hand. That was about as neat a bit of generalship on Clarke's part as any tactician could have exhibited. Old Clarke was not a bona fide lob bowler, for he could and did bowl fastish at times. He was more like Money than Drake. His two great characteristics were his judgment and his accuracy of pitch.

W.B.Money (Kent, Cambridge University, Surrey) is described by Haygarth as bowling slow twisting under-arm lobs; E.T.Drake (Cambridge University) is described as bowling under-arm lobs, twisting from the leg to the off – clearly there was a subtle difference between the two that Haygarth did not note.

Comment on Clarke's skills brings me to the unique book by Felix (Nicholas Wanostrocht) entitled *How to Play Clarke*. I believe I'm on safe ground in stating this book to be the only time that one of the principal batsmen of the day has devoted a written work trying to explain the best method of combating an outstanding bowling contemporary. Also, by contrast with today's output of cricket books, we can rest assured that Felix actually wrote every word in his book himself! There is no room to reproduce the full work here but Felix describes Clarke's bowling method thus:

> It is neither underhand, not overhand, nor round arm; nor always slow, nor ever fast; nor does it always screw from the leg to the off, but often breaks back in a contrary direction. It is varied in pitch and in pace, as much to assail the temper of the batsman, as it is meant to attack the wicket. It is, indeed, a combination of intricacies; and no man who has had the great good fortune to have made a score from him is to boast that he can play him as he likes, and where he likes. I have seen a score

How to Play Clarke:

BEING

AN ATTEMPT TO UNRAVEL THE

MYSTERIES   OF   THE   BALL,

AND TO SHOW

WHAT DEFENCE AND HITTING ARE TO BE EMPLOYED

AGAINST   THIS   CELEBRATED   BOWLER.

BY

THE   AUTHOR   OF   "FELIX   ON   THE   BAT."

LONDON:

BAILY BROTHERS,

ROYAL EXCHANGE BUILDINGS, CORNHILL.

1852.

The title page of Nicholas Felix's book – he wrote it himself – of advice to other batsmen.

of twenty runs got from his bowling, and every second hit was a bad one, made rashly, and by the merest accident in the world escaped the consequences usually attending scrambling cricket.

Clarke was aged 53 when the booklet appeared. Felix seems to have believed that there was no end to Clarke's cricketing career for he completes his book with:

If a due appreciation of one of the foregoing remarks shall cause one notch to be scored in favour of the hundred cricketers who may yet live to play against him, I shall be well rewarded for the trouble I have taken, and the great Bowler himself happy, in any suggestions which shall tend to disseminate the seeds of this chief of England sports.

William Clarke stated that he learnt more from Lambert than any man alive. In 1816, William Lambert, then the equal of any all-round cricketer in England, had published *The Instructions and Rules for Playing the*

Noble Game of Cricket. By the ninth edition, published c 1823, the book was entitled *Lambert's Cricketer's Guide*, with the original title as a subsidiary. Lambert certainly explains the art of slow bowling in some detail, so perhaps Clarke obtained a copy of the book, but the first time Clarke batted against Lambert, for Nottingham v England in 1817, Lambert bowled him for a single and the following year, in a similarly titled game, Lambert caught Clarke out.

Richard Daft described Clarke's bowling:

> Clarke's delivery was a peculiar one. He came up to the crease with the usual trot which normally all slow under-hand bowlers adopt, but instead of delivering the ball from the height of the hip, he at the last moment bent back his elbow, bringing the ball almost under his right arm pit and delivered the ball thus from as great a height as it was possible to attain and still be under-hand. He was by this delivery able to make the ball get up higher than he would have done if he had delivered in the same way as other lob bowlers. I have often heard old cricketers say that they have received many balls from Clarke which got up quite nasty from the field with a lot of screw on them. He seldom bowled two balls alike and could vary his pace and pitch in a wonderful manner.

William Caffyn, who joined the All-England Eleven towards the end of Clarke's career, reinforces Daft's remarks:

> It has been suggested that Clarke owed a great deal of his success to the fact of his appearing in public late in life, at the time when round-arm bowling had become the fashion and nearly all the great batsmen who had figured against under-hand had retired. There may be something in this, but it does not at all detract from the merit of Clarke as a bowler, for we find him, even at the close of his career, getting out regularly good batsmen who had opposed him on many occasions, and who must have become used to all his peculiarities.

With regard to his batting and fielding, Haygarth in *Scores and Biographies* makes no mention of the latter, but states: 'As a batsman he made some good scores in excellent style, hitting freely and well, though his average will not be found high, but he was often "not out".' Sutton in *Nottingham Cricket Matches from 1771 to 1853* comments: 'As a batsman, he [Clarke] is far from being inferior, but does not rank in the first-class.' Like Haygarth, Sutton does not mention Clarke's fielding abilities.

In view of the strict diets that are inflicted on today's professional cricketers, a note on Clarke's match diet is given in Ashley-Cooper's essay:

> He used to take for his lunch when playing cricket a cigar and a bottle of soda-water, which he declared were most satisfying with no after-effects of indigestion. His evening meal did not favour so Spartan a plan, for he enjoyed nothing more than a Michaelmas goose. When one was obtainable he would dine alone, and the sitting would be prolonged until little more than the bare bones of the bird remained.

Chapter Three
The 1820s

On Monday, 10 October 1831, the mob, who had been rioting through the town for a day or so, suddenly took up the cry 'To the Castle' and by the time a detachment of Hussars had been summoned and had arrived in the Castle Yard, Nottingham Castle was ablaze and beyond saving. The Castle, built between 1674 and 1679 by the first Duke of Newcastle, was nothing more than a blackened shell; it had been completely gutted.

It would be amusing to speculate that the mob had destroyed the castle because the Duke and the other major landholders in Nottinghamshire had done nothing to help the Nottingham Cricket Club during the period between 1825 and 1828 when the team had produced a series of poor results – it had been the nobility of the Dukeries who had originally introduced cricket into the County. The first reference to the game in Nottinghamshire had been of the Duke of Kingston practising cricket at Thoresby in 1751.

The speculation, however, has no basis in fact, for the mob had been infuriated by the slow passage of the great Reform Bill through the House of Lords. The area, though, seems not to have been underrepresented in Parliament. (At the time, the town of Nottingham elected two members of Parliament. The two members elected in April 1831 were Sir Thomas Denman, and General Sir Ronald Crawford Ferguson. The county also sent two members.) I should add that the Dukes of Newcastle had long since ceased to use the Castle as their residence and it was let to a number of tenants at the time of the riot.

It is, however, true that the wealthy landowners of the county, with the exception of the Charlton family of Chilwell, had nothing to do with the success or failure of the Nottingham team in the 1820s and 1830s. In the period mentioned, 1825 to 1828, Nottingham had lost five out of six major matches and Sheffield had taken over as the outstanding cricket club of the Midlands – as noted in Chapter One, Nottingham had beaten the 'far famed' Ripon Club in 1816 and England in both 1817 and 1818, then gradually faded.

With regard to the absence of support from the nobility and landed gentry, it is worth contrasting the Nottingham side of the 1820s with the professionals of the same decade in London and the south-east. The occupations of the cricketers are very revealing. The fourteen principal Nottingham players comprise five innkeepers, six lacemakers, a farmer, a weaver and a lime burner. The large majority, perhaps all, of these fifteen would, by today's definition, have been described as self-employed. I have studied a similar survey of southern professionals by checking the occupations, where known, of cricketers who represented the Players, in the annual Gentlemen v Players match staged at Lord's. The only northern player picked in the decade was Thomas Marsden of Sheffield, who began as a brickmaker, and at the end of the decade, Fuller Pilch from Norfolk. The former, probably with his earnings as the major Sheffield cricketer, moved on to be an innkeeper: the remainder of the Players came from the London area, or Kent, Surrey, Sussex and Hampshire. Five of the players were gamekeepers or bailiffs in the pay of amateur cricket enthusiasts; there were a number of tenant farmers; three players, Sparks, Bentley and Caldecourt were employed at Lord's; another was employed at Eton College. One of the few players who mirrors the Nottingham men is George Brown, with a tailoring business – it is worth noting that he moved on to take the tenancy of the Prince's Cricket Ground in Brighton, which he held from 1831 to 1840 where, just like William Clarke a few years later, Brown found running a cricket ground was not a profitable enterprise.

The Nottingham Club comprised local tradesmen and artisans, but there is no extant documentation to clarify who ran the Club, or indeed how it was organized. Reading between the lines and the odd scrap of anecdote in match reports, it would seem that the two principal figures from 1813 to 1830 were Thomas Warsop and Joe Dennis: the paragraph in Chapter One regarding the 1815 match and Dennis's financial involvement strongly suggests that Dennis led the side in that contest. Warsop, whose bowling style Clarke was reputed to have copied, is described as 'a very affable well-spoken man, by far the most gentlemanly of all the county players.' His last Nottingham match was in 1823 and he is noted elsewhere for his 'generalship'. It would be fair to assume that Warsop captained and most probably managed the Nottingham team until 1823, when gout caused his retirement; after this Dennis took over the dual role, though he had led the team in some early matches. The headquarters of the Nottingham Club would have been at that time the various inns run by Dennis – he moved from the Duke of York, York Street, to the Horse and Groom in St Peter's Square and finally the Eclipse in Chapel Bar. A stroke forced him to retire from playing in 1829 and the captaincy was taken over by Clarke; at the same time the headquarters of the Cricket Club moved to the Bell. There is a dramatic description of Dennis's final illness: 'He (Dennis) was at Clarke's house, the Bell in the Market Place, when he had another stroke, was carried on Clarke's back to his own house (about 150 yards) and died there very soon afterwards.' His death occurred on 16 November 1831 and he was buried in St Mary's two days later.

From Dennis's career one might infer that the organizer of Nottingham cricket ideally needed a public house in the centre of Nottingham – was this in Clarke's mind when he took over the Bell, having married the landlady's daughter?

From the early nineteenth century major cricket in the north of England, as has been noted, centred very largely on the Nottingham, Sheffield and Leicester sides; in the south a variety of promoters from the landed gentry class raised 'county' teams to oppose either MCC or an England Eleven selected by MCC. Surprisingly there were no major inter-county games. That all changed in 1823, when a Brighton businessman, James Ireland, took over the neglected Prince of Wales ground in the town, renaming the area as Ireland's Pleasure Grounds. He built a substantial edifice which could be used for multiple purposes and laid out a bowling green and a racquet court in addition to the actual cricket ground. Ireland selected a Sussex county side, which in 1823 played MCC home and away and, after several false starts, in 1825, home and away matches versus Kent. This latter pair of matches were the first major inter-county contests for many years and can be considered the start of the modern County Championship. If the Sussex and Kent sides of the period from 1825 are compared with the Nottingham and Sheffield teams of the same dates, the one immediate difference is that Kent and Sussex both contained a mixture of amateurs and professionals, whereas both Nottingham and Sheffield sides were almost exclusively composed of professionals. This difference would continue over the next hundred years and establish, in a manner of speaking, the 'North-South' divide.

Reverting to the Nottingham Club, no matches were played in 1819 or 1820; in 1821 Holt Cricket Club challenged Nottingham to a match to be played at Holt. The Norfolk side offered to pay Nottingham's travelling expenses and the challenge was accepted. Holt scored 80 and 73; Nottingham 150 and then hit off the four runs required for victory without losing a wicket. William Clarke scored seven and bowled out five Holt batsmen in their second innings. In the press the match was advertised for 240 guineas (i.e. 120 guineas a side), which, if true, made the trip profitable for the Nottingham men.

In August, what are described as 'Eleven of the favourite and experienced players of the Cropwell and Bingham Clubs' opposed twenty-two of the Fallowfield Club. Someone named Clarke with no initial plays for the eleven, but does little and the eleven are defeated; the match was played 'near' Colston Bassett. As mentioned before it is doubtful whether the Cropwell Clarkes are directly connected to William.

Commencing on 10 September, Eleven of the Nottingham Club played Sixteen of the whole of the county of Leicester in Abbey Meadow, Leicester, not the usual field. The Nottingham press seem more interested in the fact that William Charlton Esq of Chilwell agreed to umpire and reported that 'William Charlton was umpire all three days and from every quarter we have heard the most handsome testimonies to his great attention, his quick discernment and his gentlemanly conduct.' William Charlton was High Sheriff of Nottingham in 1824; his son, T.B.Charlton (1815-1886) played for Nottinghamshire in 1840.

Clarke's ability as a batsman was apparent with innings of seven and 18, and though the figures of course look modest by later standards, both proved the highest for Nottingham; the team were all out for 24 and 56. They lost by an innings. Leicester then challenged Nottingham to an eleven-a-side match at Loughborough: Nottingham accepted, but later withdrew from the contest.

In October it was reported that William Clarke was involved in a single-wicket match. The game was played on The Forest, William Clarke and John Hewitt opposing five of the New Radford Club. Clarke scored nine and none, Hewitt four and four, but New Radford made 16 in their first innings and their opening bat, Charles Howitt, completed the match by hitting the two runs required for victory. The last mention of William Clarke in 1821 came in a match on 18, 19 and 22 October on the Nottingham Cricket Ground when he scored 16 and one for a combined Cropwell and Bingham eleven v sixteen of the Fallowfield Club. Clarke's 16 was the highest score in the combined side's first innings. As before, though, is this our William Clarke?

The first Nottingham match of 1822 was staged on The Forest v the Norfolk club of Holt for £100. Nottingham won by 105 runs; William Clarke is shown as opening the batting for Nottingham – only seven Holt wickets fell 'bowled' out of the twenty: Clarke took three of the seven.

The two major Nottingham games of the year were home and away against Sheffield, Nottingham allowing Sheffield fifteen men against the Nottingham eleven. Both produced overwhelming victories for Nottingham – by 10 wickets and by an innings and 113 runs. In the latter match Clarke again opened the Nottingham batting and this time made the highest score of 45, though he is not credited with any wickets in either match.

The Sheffield match was the first important game staged on George Steer's ground at Darnall. The public interest was overwhelming and a temporary grandstand to accommodate 2,000 people was erected for the occasion. Unfortunately the structure was not capable of such a crowd and collapsed on the first afternoon. Initial reports gave two dead and 50 injured, but later these figures were reduced to 17 admitted to the Infirmary – there were no deaths. The press stated that the matches were each played for 60 sovereigns. On The Forest, a curious incident was reported – Thomas Warsop was judged out by the umpire for stopping the ball with his bat, when it had been thrown in; the note also adds 'his running was defective owing to gout'.

Thomas Warsop at the time was considered one of only two Nottingham players – the other being Joe Dennis – who, given the right inducement, wouldn't sell a match. Warsop was down to play in the match at Holt in 1821, but owing to gout was reduced to being a spectator. The following story is told of an incident concerning Warsop during the game. He had, as a mere *façon de parler*, a habit of saying, 'Done with you for a hundred,' which of course was properly estimated by his friends, but, like his bowling, was misleading to a stranger. After lunch on the second day, Warsop was in a group drinking wine – not recommended for gout. One of the Holt supporters exclaimed, 'Why, we shall beat you Nottingham gents yet.' Warsop responded, 'Done with you for a hundred.' On the third day Nottingham won by ten wickets; the Holt gentleman handed over twenty 'fivers' to Warsop, but was immediately told, 'Oh, pooh, pooh, take your money back; I was only in jest, and should certainly not have thought of paying you had Nottingham lost.'

The scale of the successes that attended Nottingham in their matches with Sheffield in 1822 meant that the two adversaries would not play each other again until 1827. As is clearly demonstrated, matches were played for stake money and Sheffield players couldn't risk stakes on what immediately after 1822 looked like a hopeless case.

There are a number of matches reported in the Nottingham press following the Nottingham v Sheffield game on The Forest; none feature William Clarke, but one game is significant in view of future events. On 11 October, the *Nottingham Review* reported: 'On Friday last a match at Cricket in a field near Trent Bridge was played between Mr Samuel Chapman at the Three Horse Shoes & Crown Inn with ten of his men against XI of the West Bridgford Club.' Chapman's side comprised S.Chapman, G.Chapman, C.Singlehurst, E.Singlehurst, J.Selby sen, J.Selby jun, G.Selby, W.Jackson, J.Jackson, T.Horsley and C.Humphries. The Three Horse Shoes and Crown Inn later changed its name to the Trent Bridge Inn. Samuel Chapman was married to Mary Singlehurst, who was to marry William Clarke in 1837. The implications of the marriage will form part of a later chapter, but the question raised by this match is whether it was played on the field that is now Trent Bridge Cricket Ground – it could well have been played in an adjacent meadow. It is impossible to answer the question, though it is an intriguing one!

Perhaps here we should note, by way of a diversion, one non-cricketing reference to Clarke in 1822; it occurs in the *Nottingham Review* of 26 July, advertising 'A Gooseberry Show at Mr Clarke's The Bell Inn, Angel Row'. What do they know of cricket who only cricket know?

The first sporting reference, other than horse racing, in the Nottingham press for the summer of 1823 is dated 6 June: 'Clarke and Simpson of Nottingham opposed Jeffries and Shreves of Birmingham at fives on Tuesday – Nottingham won five games to nil.' All the detailed biographies of Clarke note that he was an expert fives player, but lost the sight of an eye when hit by a fives 'between 1820 and 1830'. At least this 1823 report narrows the time span a little. It would seem that little or no research has been done into the playing of fives in Nottingham, or indeed into the game of fives in any real depth. From what we know of Clarke it would seem likely that he would play fives professionally but William Caffyn in his reminiscences makes the following comment: 'He [Clarke] would play fives for hours together, and made such hard work of it that when he leaned exhausted against the wall of the fives court he often left a sort of silhouette of himself in perspiration on the wall!' It is believed that Clarke had a fives court at the rear of the Bell Inn.

The Nottingham Club played just two matches in 1823. The first was against XXII of the Fallowfield Club (also described as XXII of the South of the County). Opening the innings William Clarke scored 23 – again the highest score of the entire match. The opposition was weak, Nottingham winning by seven wickets – the three-day game was played on The Forest.

The second Nottingham match was played on The Forest against fourteen of Leicester for 60 guineas, commencing on 25 August. Clarke batted at No.4, but the feature of the match was an innings by Joe Dennis. If the second-innings order is correct, Dennis opened and was still unbeaten with 50 not out when the last wicket fell. The report comments: 'Dennis was in more than three hours and had so got into the spirit of the game that the ball seemed to fly to and from his bat as though it had been a magic wand.' Clarke does not feature in any of the six local club matches published in the Nottingham press during 1823.

There are no recorded Nottingham Club matches in 1824 – one assumes no club within travelling distance would risk challenging Nottingham. Bingham, however, challenged Sheffield to a match on 4 August for reportedly 100 sovereigns, but suffered in consequence, being beaten by eight wickets. Four regular Nottingham Club players, including Clarke, reinforced the Bingham team – Clarke scored nought and nine. This match has importance locally being the only time Bingham attempted to challenge such notable opponents. It was the first game to be played on Mr Steer's enlarged and improved venue at Darnall and it was the first recorded match in which the soon-to-be-famous Tom Marsden appeared. He bowled out eleven Bingham batsmen and made Sheffield's highest score.

With no nearby opponents and having overwhelmed Holt (or in another version, Norfolk), Nottingham had little option but to cast their net wider and challenged Bury St Edmunds in 1825. Matters did not go smoothly. Three successive weekly editions of the *Bury and Norwich Post* reported on the negotiations. On 31 August it stated, 'A grand cricket match for £100 a side between the Bury and Nottingham Clubs will be played at Rougham, near this town before the season's over. The day and other particulars we shall be able to state in our next.' On 7 September, it noted that 'The grand Match of Cricket for £100 a side between the Bury and Nottingham Clubs will be played at Rougham, near this town on Monday next. As the Bury Club is to have the assistance of Messrs Brand and Mathews and another Gentleman from Suffolk and as the Nottingham players are very celebrated, the Match excites the greatest interest.' Finally on 14 September: 'Owing to a demur on the part of the Nottingham Club the great match of Cricket which was to have commenced on Monday at Rougham near this town was declared "off" and it was not until two o'clock that a new arrangement of terms was completed. In consequence of this delay only one innings was played that evening, in which the Bury side scored 76. The Nottingham men went in at ten o'clock yesterday morning, but the match was not expected to be finished in the day.'

The newspaper for 21 September then gives a detailed account of the game. In essence, Nottingham claimed they did not realize that such famous players as Brand and Mathews were going to take part. Bury agreed to reduce the stake from £100 to £40 and to pay Nottingham £20 towards their expenses. The betting commenced at 5 to 4 against Bury, but when Bury obtained a lead of 23 after the first innings, the odds were changed to 3 to 2 in favour of Bury. However, Bury lost cheap early wickets in their second innings and at the close of the second day the betting was nearly even. Clarke scored two and 13 (out of 53 and 78) and bowled down six wickets. The report continues: 'The play on all sides was admitted equal to any ever seen in Lord's Ground, the bowling being in no wise inferior. This you knew was the opinion of Mr Brand, who expressed himself delighted with the game.'

John Brand first played at Lord's (for MCC) in 1815 and from 1819 to 1823 appeared for the Gentlemen v Players at Lord's. His estate was near Ipswich, though he was born in Armenia, compiling a dictionary of that country's language. Haygarth describes Brand 'as a successful batsman for about 15 seasons in the great contests of the day.' Sadly he died on 29 April 1856 in a lunatic asylum, in which he had been confined for some time. William Mathews was employed by John Brand as a gamekeeper on the family's estate, having moved there not long before the match in question – Nottingham were therefore probably right to query Mathews' qualification for Bury or Suffolk. He was, according to Haygarth, the first bowler to bowl slow round-arm and had a few summers of great success, though his gamekeeping job ended in 1830, when Brand's health began to decline. He took an inn in Woodbridge and died there in 1858.

Clarke's name is not to be found in any other local matches during 1825. The following summer, despite their defeat at the hands of Bury, Nottingham had the audacity to challenge, for the first time, the combined strengths of Sheffield and Leicester. The match was staged at Darnall on 24, 25 and 26 July 1826. Interest in the match was great – according to the *Sheffield Mercury* 25,000 spectators attended over the three days, or 30,000 in another account. The combined team won by the vast margin of an innings and 203 runs, almost entirely due to one player, Tom Marsden, who hit 227. The detailed score of this match was discovered a few years ago in the Sheffield Archives office by Steve Bilton and copied out by Mick Pope. It is the earliest known document which gives the full bowling analysis for a match – Barker and Clarke opened the Nottingham attack and the latter returned figures of 76.3-13-161-5. Marsden took eight for 76 in the two innings and had it not been for him, surely Nottingham would have proved the winners. The match was for 200 sovereigns.

Thomas Barker was an exact contemporary of Clarke, both having been born in 1798. In contrast to Clarke, Barker's delivery was most impetuous. Denison notes: 'So violent was it, that he sometimes ran up to the crease and propelled the instrument of attack as though his head would follow the ball.' His career almost ended when he was travelling to Southampton to play against Hampshire in 1843. Taking a cab whilst changing stations in London, the horse bolted and Barker broke his leg as he leapt from the vehicle.

After the catastrophic defeat at the hands of the combined Sheffield and Leicester team, Nottingham arranged home and away matches with the Sheffield Club in both 1827 and 1828, but lost three out of the four meetings. These reverses were very largely due to the efforts of Tom

Marsden. He was top scorer for Sheffield in five of the eight innings played and hit another three-figure score on The Forest in the 1828 game – 125 out of a Sheffield total of 220.

In the match on The Forest in 1827, the *Nottingham Review* reported: 'Jefferies, the Nottingham umpire, no-balled Marsden for jerking the ball, so frequently that the Sheffield players left the field.' Play was not resumed until 4 o'clock when Nottingham agreed to replace Jefferies with William Taylor of Radcliffe. Whether the term 'jerk' in this context is intended to mean bowling above elbow height it is not possible to determine. As noted in the previous chapter the phrasing 'thrown or jerked' was introduced in the 1816 version of the bowling Laws. Haygarth describes Marsden as 'very fast under-arm and round-arm of moderate speed'.

There seem to be strict regulations governing the qualification of players in these Nottingham v Sheffield games – Emmanuel Vincent, who had lived in Nottingham 'for some time', but was a native of Sheffield, was not allowed to appear for Nottingham, but was permitted to do so the following year.

Clarke was easily the outstanding all-rounder during these matches. His bowling down of 16 wickets was the most by any Nottingham bowler and his total of 91 runs was only exceeded by George Jarvis. Jarvis (1800-1880) was the first Nottingham Club player to be selected for an England team, appearing at Darnall in the 1827 England v Sussex match. He later played five times for the Players v Gentlemen at Lord's.

The match with Sheffield on 1, 2 and 3 September 1828 is of historical interest, the *Nottingham Review* stating: 'Mr J.Dennis declined to play and T.Heath substituted, so that the whole of the "Old First Eleven" as they are called have now done with playing. Thomas Warsop stood umpire with William Charlton of Chilwell.'

The great match of 1828 was All-England v Three Counties at Darnall on 8, 9 and 10 September. Clarke, with Barker, Jarvis and Vincent, were the Nottingham representatives in the Counties' eleven (Leicestershire, Nottinghamshire and Yorkshire), but the round-arm bowling of Broadbridge and Lillywhite utterly routed the Counties – all out 60 and 32, with England winning by 242 runs. Sheffield contributed five players and Leicester two. Clarke took a single wicket bowled, and scored six and two. The game was considered a direct forerunner of the first 'official' North v South match and was a desperate attempt by the owner of the Darnall Ground to boost its image – very shortly a newly developed ground in Sheffield 'Hyde Park' would take over as the town's principal cricket venue.

Chapter Four
Onward and Upward

In 1829 the Nottingham Club, for the first time, arranged home and away fixtures with both Sheffield and Leicester, plus a revival of the Town v County fixture on The Forest – perhaps a further indication that William Clarke had assumed the leadership of the town club.

Clarke appeared mainly as a batsman in the 1829 games, the main attack being Redgate, Barker (both fast round-arm) and the Mansfield cricketer John Hilton, described by Sutton as 'the most remarkable of all bowlers', but we have no elucidation as to why. He bowled slow round-arm. Clarke scarcely bowled at all.

On 21 February 1830 the last of William Clarke's children, Alfred, was baptised at St Nicholas' Church, Nottingham. The eldest child, Frances, had died in 1827, but Alfred had two living brothers and two sisters – John (b 1823), Matilda (b 1824), William (b 1826) and Jane (b 1828). Alfred was to become a useful county cricketer, but nowhere near as prominent as his father.

The only Nottingham match of the season was with Sheffield on their new ground at Hyde Park – for 100 sovereigns. Prior to the game, a practice match was organized on The Forest between the Nottingham first eleven and the next twenty-two; Clarke's innings of 27 was the highest in the match and again the first-eleven bowling was dominated by Barker and Redgate who bowled down 12 wickets between them. In the match at Hyde Park, Clarke repeated his feat of the highest innings, 59, but his colleagues failed against the bowling of Marsden, who took ten wickets bowled in the match and scored 48. Sheffield won by 41 runs. It was Clarke's first fifty in 'first-class' cricket.

The brief Nottingham Club programme for 1830 was repeated in 1831. Nottingham's first eleven opposed T.Heath and twenty-one selected by him from the town and neighbourhood. The eleven made 121, with wides contributing 23 – an indication of round-arm being employed – whilst Heath's team were all out for 88. As a prelude to the Sheffield match at Hyde Park, Clarke, Jarvis and Barker challenged three of Sheffield (namely Smith, Rawlins and Marsden) to a single-wicket match. Barker bowled down five of the wickets and caught the sixth: Sheffield made eight and 13. Nottingham scored 31 (Clarke 12, Jarvis 12, Barker 7). Exactly why the Nottingham v Sheffield match was arranged for Hyde Park for a second successive year is, I assume, a matter of money: the proprietor, who was the son-in-law of Mr Steer who ran the Darnall ground, could charge admission, which Nottingham, at home, couldn't. The owner of the ground did well, with 7,000 attending the second day's play. Nottingham won by 125 runs. Clarke bowled down five and scored 18 and 17.

One of the great matches of the season at Lord's was England v The Bs – despite his obvious ability, Barker was not in the Bs eleven and no Nottingham men were seen in the Players v Gentlemen side of that year.

In 1832, for a third year in succession, the Nottingham v Sheffield game was played at Hyde Park. The *Nottingham Review*, which in 1831 had in its Nottingham v Sheffield report the bald statement: 'Clarke bowled well', did, in 1832, become slightly more effusive: 'Clarke never bowled better and it would have been hardly possible for him to have given straighter balls as he would in every instance with, we believe, one exception, have taken a wicket – it took Tom Marsden one hour to get seven in the first innings and an hour and a half to get 18 in the second.' Economically 1832 was a bad year, perhaps the first downturn since the end of the Napoleonic Wars, hence perhaps the rioting in major towns.

In view of the comment on Clarke's bowling, it is worth looking at the printed scorecard, which credits Clarke with just one wicket, out of 20, bowled down – one assumes that many, if not most, of the eight Sheffield wickets that fell in the first innings, other than bowled, must have been taken by Clarke. Nottingham won by 153 runs. The report concluded with: 'Clarke did not bowl in the second innings, having to return to Nottingham owing to a serious illness in the family.'

The growing importance of William Clarke as the organizer of Nottingham cricket is further emphasized by the note in the *Nottingham Review* of 24 August 1832: 'Tom Heath of Nottingham challenges anyone from Leicestershire for £10 to £20 – Apply Clarke's, The Bell Inn, Angel Row, Nottingham.'

The first Nottingham game of note in 1833 is a single-wicket match, Three of Nottingham v Three of Sheffield. Marsden completely dominates the proceedings taking all six Nottingham wickets, including Clarke for none in both innings and then Marsden scores 12. The Nottingham trio are dismissed for 7 and 3 – all ten runs being scored by Jarvis, the third of the trio; Barker also recorded a pair. The unusual aspect of the game was the location, described as 'On the New Ground, Hulme, near Manchester'. It supposedly lasted three days and certainly scoring was painfully slow. Marsden faced 280 balls (70 overs) for his 12, whilst Jarvis in his second innings faced 111 balls for 3 runs. Was the match financially rewarding for the owner of the new ground?

The single foreign fixture by the Nottingham Club was against a twenty of Ripon, York, Wetherby, Bedale, Thirsk and Harewood (or in another version, Yorkshire bar Sheffield). The last time that Ripon had been involved was a twelve-a-side contest (Clarke's debut) in 1816, Nottingham winning by an innings. The game in 1833 was drawn owing to a dispute that arose when Strickland of the twenty was judged 'run out'. From the historical viewpoint, the Nottingham Club eleven included two amateurs. Nottingham had included one of the amateurs, George Rothera, in the

1832 match away against Sheffield; he was a member of a well-known family connected to the legal profession in Nottingham. Rothera played in the Ripon game and this time his fellow amateur was George Galloway, a hosiery manufacturer in partnership with his brother, John, and in 1842 a member of the Town Council. Thereafter good, and occasionally not so good, amateur cricketers were sometimes included in the Nottingham team, especially for away matches in order to help with the expenses – this point was to become more evident in the 1840s.

Two weeks after the Ripon match there was a game between Nottingham (who went to Ripon) and the Next XXII, which the report notes was arranged because it was felt that the strongest possible Nottingham side had not been picked for the match at Ripon. The report continues: 'The "metal" of both sides was excited much more than in an ordinary match.' The XXII won by two wickets. The match was played for £10-a-side.

Clarke felt confident enough to expand the horizons of the Nottingham Club and on 2 May 1834 issued challenges to the counties of Norfolk, Cambridgeshire and Hertfordshire – an interesting trio. Norfolk had opposed Yorkshire at Hyde Park, Sheffield in 1833; Cambridge Town Club played the University in two matches in 1833; and Hertfordshire (mainly the Grimston family) played occasionally against MCC, including one in 1835. In the event only Cambridge accepted the challenge.

Clarke arranged two very curious 'trial' games, as well as the usual Town v County fixture before tackling Cambridge. The first of these was against Bingham, the village being allowed four innings to Nottingham's two. Clarke dominated the two Town v County fixtures, scoring 26 and 40, the two highest innings in both games, which were single-innings fixtures. These Bingham games were advertised as for £50: Nottingham won both contests. In between the two matches Clarke challenged seven of West Bridgford to a single-wicket match in West Bridgford. Clarke scored 23 and then dismissed all seven for 7 and 10! In the West Bridgford team is S.Chapman, who is most probably Samuel Chapman, the 22-year-old son of Mary Chapman, widow and landlady of the Trent Bridge Inn.

The great matches against Cambridge proved an anticlimax, though 10,000 spectators turned out for the first day of play on The Forest. Nottingham won at Cambridge by 152 runs and on The Forest by an innings and 114 runs. As the Forest match ended in a day and a half, a second game between Cambridge and the New Forest Club was played. In this Clarke scored 42 of New Forest's 121 and Cambridge were 18 for three when the game ended.

Despite the fives accident which deprived Clarke of the sight of one eye, he was still keen to claim his expertise at this sport, as a notice in the *Stamford Mercury* of 14 November 1834 makes clear, though there seems to be no record of a response: 'Mr Clarke of the Bell Inn, Nottingham, the famous cricket player, has given a public challenge to play any man in England a game at fives for £50.'

Very few New Forest Club matches were published in the local papers in the 1830s and this may account for the fact that William Clarke's name rarely features in local club games at this time. Two years later on 5 October 1835 in the *Nottingham Observer* the following notice was printed:

On Tuesday last members of the New Forest Club held their concluding field-day meeting for the season, on the Nottingham Ground, but the sports of the day were brought to a speedy conclusion by the unfavourable state of the weather. The party then adjourned to Mr William Clarke's, the Bell Inn, Nottingham, where an excellent dinner was provided, and Mr Clarke invited to join them. After the cloth was drawn, the chairman (the President of the club) presented to Mr Clarke an excellent silver snuff-box: it was wrought very beautifully and the following inscription was engraved on the lid: 'Presented to Mr Wm. Clarke by the members of the New Forest Club, as a memorial of esteem for his kind services in the practice of the game of Cricket, and as umpire on many occasions. September 1835.' Mr Clarke returned thanks in a suitable address, and the social board closed the day's amusement.

Chapter Five
First Matches with Sussex and the Consequences

Having thoroughly disposed of Cambridge(shire), Clarke immediately began to explore the possibility of playing the two outstanding cricketing counties, Kent and Sussex. Purely due to the efforts of James Ireland, the proprietor of the principal Brighton cricket ground (founded in the 1790s by the Prince of Wales), Kent began playing Sussex, home and away, in 1825. In 1827, the press announced that whichever of the two counties won that year would 'take the Championship Belt', a direct reference to the belts often awarded to successful boxers. As previously noted, it was the origin of the inter-county competition. Before that time aspiring county sides (or their patrons) had one basic aim, to beat the combined strength of England, an ambition that goes back at least to the famous Kent v England match on the Artillery Ground in London in 1744. (Nottingham had made several attempts to beat England, notably in 1817 and 1818, but had fielded twenty-two players against eleven.)

However, by 1835 no northern county had single-handedly challenged any of the southern counties, Kent, Sussex, Surrey or Hampshire. Kent lacked cohesion, the strength being split between two or three centres. The county had, however, played England twice in 1834, the home game being at Chislehurst. Then, in 1835, a local cricket enthusiast and patron, Thomas Selby, engaged Fuller Pilch at Town Malling – these days usually known as West Malling – and for several years this town became the Kent headquarters. Pilch made his Kent debut at Town Malling v Sussex in 1836. Surrey and Hampshire in 1835 were both in abeyance: Surrey wouldn't revive until the creation of Kennington Oval as a headquarters in 1846; Hampshire found a suitable ground in Southampton and a suitable groundkeeper in Daniel Day, the latter in 1842, but the County Club was, to say the least, unstable.

George Brown, the famous Sussex cricketer, took over Ireland's Ground, the Brighton venue, in 1831 and was keen to promote matches on the ground – his enthusiasm naturally increased when the notable round-arm pioneer, William Lillywhite, took control of a second ground in the town, threatening Brown's effective monopoly. Brighton was mirroring Sheffield where, as mentioned, the Darnall Ground lost out to Hyde Park in the 1820s. Brown was therefore very keen that the Nottingham side should come to Brighton and play on his ground – from Clarke's viewpoint the whole venture fell nicely into place.

The match in Brighton proved to be a battle of the round-arm bowlers:

Broadbridge and Lillywhite were the Sussex round-armers, Barker and Redgate were Nottinghamshire's. Several commentators have made the point that Clarke, as captain, tended to hog the bowling and not know when to rest, but in this case, and in the return fixture, he did not put himself on to bowl – a very unusual situation. However the report on the Brighton game states:

> Barker is a good hand at every department of the game – bowling fielding and batting. He delivers his balls with great swiftness, their force being added to by his height and the spring which he gives before doing so. His strength must be very great to enable him to undergo such exertion as he did on this day. Redgate's bowling was at first tremendous and hardly to be resisted but evidently slackened as the day advanced. On the whole we prefer the bowling of Barker to Redgate.

Barker took six wickets, Redgate four on the first day, with Sussex all out for 94. In the second innings Barker and Redgate shared the wickets and Nottinghamshire (so called, rather than Nottingham) won by two wickets. They required seven to win with eight wickets down at the second day's close. The one adverse comment in the Nottingham papers was: 'Nottinghamshire have no good wicket-keeper, several players taking this place.'

The return match on The Forest was immortalized by William Howitt in his book *Rural Life in England*. His vivid description of this match and the whole atmosphere of cricket on The Forest was reprinted in detail in F.S.Ashley-Cooper's *Nottinghamshire Cricket and Cricketers* in 1923 and again in Christopher Lee's history of Sussex cricket *From The Sea End* (1989). A brief extract will convey the whole:

> Along each side of the ground ran a bank sloping down to it, and it, and the booths, and the tents at the ends were occupied with a dense mass of people, all as silent as the ground beneath them; and all up the hill were groups, and on the race-stand an eager, forward-leaning throng. There were said to be twenty thousand people, all hushed as death, except when some exploit of the players produced a thunder of applause. ... But nothing was so beautiful as the sudden shout, the rush, and breaking up of the crowd, when the last decisive notch was gained.

There is a very full report of this historic game in the *Nottingham Review*. Again Clarke did not bowl and apart from a few overs from Billy Good, Barker and Redgate formed the attack. Unfortunately for Sussex Lillywhite was unable to play, a great loss to them. Nottinghamshire's batting was saved by Billy Good who made the highest score in both innings and was 20 not out when Notts won by three wickets. These two Sussex matches were the only two external matches played by Nottingham in 1835.

The nomenclature of the Nottingham side perhaps requires some explanation. A Nottinghamshire County Cricket Club did not exist – in fact in 1835 there were no organizations claiming to be a 'County Cricket Club', even in Sussex and Kent, the two counties that had regularly played matches for the past decade. The *Nottingham Review* of 24 April 1835 contains the first report of cricket in the county that summer with: 'The season commenced with a practice Match of Nottingham Old Cricket Club: Town v County.' The detailed score then follows. The term 'Nottingham Old Club' seems to first appear in William North's book of scores published in 1830. The book is dedicated thus: 'To the Gentlemen of the Nottingham Old Cricket Club and to the Admirers of the Noble Game of Cricket.' Prior to that the main cricket eleven in the town went just by the name Nottingham Club.

There was no immediate follow-up to the successes against Sussex, despite the following note in the *Nottingham Review* of 10 June 1836: 'We understand that Sussex wish to play Nottinghamshire and hope steps will be taken to arrange a match.'

The now usual Town v County game was played in late May. Billy Good was not available, engaged at Lord's, nor was Sam Redgate, engaged at Cambridge. A young amateur, Charles Creswell, was brought in to replace Redgate and was described as bowling with 'great precision'.

The cricket season was dominated by an MCC proposal for two matches between the North of England and the South. The first match was arranged to take place at Lord's on 11, 12 and 13 July. No definite decision was taken regarding the return match, save that it was to be in the North. For the initial fixture six Nottingham men – Barker, Jarvis, Clarke, Good, Redgate and Creswell – were picked; two from Sheffield, Marsden and Vincent (Vincent had returned to that town in 1833); two from Cambridge, Fenner and D.Hayward; plus Fuller Pilch from Norfolk. The North won by six wickets – Barker, Redgate and Creswell took all the South wickets. There is no indication that Clarke bowled, but it was Clarke's first match at Lord's. Who captained the North is not mentioned in the reports. The match was played for £500 and one of the major promoters of the North was Capt Richard Cheslyn, Leicestershire-born and a fair club cricketer. Eric Snow in *A History of Leicestershire Cricket* points out that some years later a job was found for him, when 'betting losses had brought him down in the world.'

Cheslyn persuaded MCC that the return match should be played at Leicester. This fact produced a violent reaction from the Nottingham press on 16 July:

The return match has been fixed to be played at Leicester on Monday the 22d of August, which has given universal dissatisfaction, nay, even disgust, to the supporters and admirers of the game in Nottingham and its neighbourhood, and well it may, for who is the party to be benefitted by the match being played there? Is he a cricketer? No! Has he furnished or has the town and county furnished a player in the late match? No! Has the game of cricket been better or longer supported at Leicester than at Nottingham? We answer 'No!' Have the players been in the habit of treating their opponents with greater courtesy or civility than at Nottingham? In giving an answer to this, we confidently assert, 'No!' Then what is it that has caused Leicester to be fixed upon? This, we confess, we are unable to answer, unless it be that Leicester is possessed of a walled-in ground, made upon speculation, which created a tax upon cricketers and the admirers of the game and which we know to have failed entirely, as matches played in such places have ever been looked upon with suspicion for there have been so many got up for the mere purpose of remunerating the owners of them; besides they almost totally exclude the majority of the most fervent admirers and practisers of the game. Such places and the system above mentioned have almost annihilated the game in several towns; look for instance at Sheffield, but more particularly at Leicester fixed upon for the return match to be played at, whilst at Nottingham, it has been steadily progressing till it has arrived at the pitch that they are competent to play any county in England. Having said thus much to show that Leicester is not entitled to the precedence we will offer a few remarks which we trust will show that on Nottingham and it alone ought the choice to have been made. In the first place Nottingham has for more than half a century stood very high in the annals of cricketing. We have chronicled matches as far back as 1771 since which time they have been played and been practiced by the principal players in 59 matches, 34 of which they have won. [A list of opponents etc is added here.]

To Mr Clarke, who has spared neither time nor expense in forwarding and supporting this noble game, assisted by the noblemen and gentlemen (though few, very few, we are sorry to say of that class are to be found amongst supporters of cricket in this neighbourhood) the tradesmen and mechanics of the town; who by their combined efforts have been enabled to furnish SIX players in the late match, and have it in their power to send a SEVENTH to the return match, we would, we hesitate not, to materially improve the eleven; and yet forsooth it is to be played at Leicester from which place not even one has been sent. Is this the reward the people of Nottingham are to receive for having contributed so much to the advancement of that most noble and manly of all games? For the character of the conduct exhibited by the spectators on such occasions as the ground is open, we can with confidence refer to Lord Beauclerk and E.H.Budd Esq., who played here in 1817, when there could not have been less than fifteen thousand present to witness the match. We hope and trust that our townsmen will lose no time but bestir themselves and by a proper and timely representation being made at headquarters that the place may yet be changed for Nottingham.'

The public meeting urged by the newspaper duly took place at the Exchange Hall. With a resolution produced stating that the Meeting should consider the best means to be adopted to 'induce the Noblemen and Gentlemen who superintend the arrangements connected with the match between the Counties North and South of the Thames to select Nottingham as the place for playing the Return Game on the 22nd of August 1836.' The chair was taken by the Mayor of Nottingham. Three resolutions were passed supporting Nottingham as the venue and these were forwarded to the Secretary of MCC, Benjamin Aislabie, through Mr John Hicklin, proprietor of the *Nottingham Journal*. The reply simply stated that an agreement had already been made to play at Leicester, but MCC were happy to consider Nottingham for any future match.

So the match took place on the Wharf Street Ground at Leicester. A great many Nottingham cricket supporters went to Leicester for the game – some had to make the journey on foot as all the available horse-drawn transport was booked up. Other Nottingham supporters found all the accommodation in Leicester was taken and had to seek bed and lodgings overnight in Loughborough. There were numerous complaints in the Nottingham newspapers. These were compounded by the following report in the *Leicester Herald*:

> Every one seemed gratified if we except the Nottingham visitors. ... Lillywhite was rather unsuccessful with the bat, but he made amends in knocking down the consequences of the Nottingham players, several of whom we consider only second-raters. It was drily observed at the termination of this innings, that 'had the match been played on the Sands at Nottingham, not one of the South players would have been allowed to return into Kent and Sussex to tell the tale'. Upon the whole we feel delighted at the issue, for it has done one thing, lowered the pride of the Nottingham players. They appeared to us complete second-rates, and when matched by the beautiful fielding of the South had very little chance indeed. They must never again think of calling a public meeting at Nottingham, with the Mayor in the Chair, and talk such nonsense and fulsome stuff about the invulnerable players of Nottingham. They may challenge a county town but Sussex and Kent are too much for them.

The Leicester newspapers don't appear to acknowledge the fact that Barker (who took 11 wickets at Lord's) was unable to bowl due to a sprain: he did, though, open the batting for the North. The South won by 218 runs, William Lillywhite taking 11 wickets in the match, but the star of the game was Alfred Mynn, the Kent amateur, who hit 125 not out in the second innings. Mynn had damaged his leg in practice prior to his innings and should not have batted. This was in the days before pads – Redgate's fast deliveries hit him on the damaged leg on several occasions (Mynn employed a runner). So badly bruised was the leg that he was unable to play again for over a year. Would he have survived so long at the crease if Barker had bowled in harness with Redgate?

In consequence of the use of Leicester as the venue, Clarke declined to play; he hadn't bowled at Lord's and his place was taken by William Garrat, who won praise for his batting at Leicester: 'The batting of Garrat we cannot refrain from noticing, it was admired by everyone and his runs were got in a masterly style' (*Nottingham Review*). Also missing from the Northern eleven at Leicester were the two Cambridge players, their places being occupied by the Nottingham amateur George Rothera, and James Dearman of Sheffield.

Chapter Six
Fate Takes a Hand

As a result of the 1836 North v South matches, Clarke was not slow to take up the MCC offer of a North v South match at Nottingham. On 26 May 1837 the *Nottingham Review* announced: 'Amongst various matches arranged this season is Nottinghamshire and Yorkshire with Box and Cobbett against England at Lord's with a return at Nottingham.' On the same date, the paper has a second cricket notice:

> A Public Meeting was held at the Poultry Hotel last Tuesday to calculate the expenses incurred in playing two matches with Sussex. A highly respectable committee with power to add to their number was nominated to collect the necessary subscriptions and it was agreed to apply by letter to the patrons of this manly exercise among the nobility and gentry of the County.

(In view of the opinion expressed in the newspaper article of 15 July 1836 it is rather quaint to read that the nobility and gentry are to be bombarded with cricket begging letters - no more seems to have been heard of this 'respectable committee', but in 1840 some amateurs were drafted into the county side so perhaps the meeting produced positive results, though no extant details seem to materialize until 1841.)

The Sussex fixtures were arranged for Brighton (Brown's Ground) on 24 July and for The Forest on 21 August. Sussex developed from collecting a list of subscribers for match expenses in 1836 to a full-blown Sussex County Cricket Club operating from the start of the 1839 season. Why the good folk of Nottingham did not immediately follow the same course, will become quite obvious as the events of the next decade unfold and it was not until 1859 that a fully functioning organization became properly established, though there were attempts and earlier flimsy clubs prior to that year.

The 1837 season in Nottingham opened with a match on The Forest on 5 June, incidentally a few days before the accession of Queen Victoria, aged 18, to the throne. The game was between eleven of the New Forest Club with Barker and Jarvis given against 'the best eleven that Mr Clarke can field from the Town and County'. The New Forest Club scored 147 of which Tom Barker made 62 and George Jarvis 23. In reply what, in the press, is entitled the Old Club made 121 with Joe Guy scoring 20. A note appended to the score states that Deakin, a Leicester player, was bowling in place of Barker. Why, we don't know. Barker had been unable to bowl in the North v South game at Leicester.

On 3 July on The Forest, Sixteen picked by Clarke opposed Eleven picked by Barker. Jarvis, Good and Redgate were unavailable being engaged that week at Lord's. The infamous Gentlemen v Players 'Barn Door' match was being played at Lord's on the same date.

The following week the advertised Nottinghamshire and Yorkshire with Cobbett and Box v England match took place at Lord's. It was now titled North v South and was being played to celebrate the fiftieth anniversary of the founding of Lord's first Ground in 1787. There is no doubt that 1837 was the fiftieth anniversary of Thomas Lord founding his original ground on the site of what is now Dorset Square, but the North v South match was also billed as the fiftieth anniversary of the Marylebone Club, a point that causes today's historians heart-ache. The Cricket Club, which asked Lord to find a piece of land suitable for the Club, had its origins many years before. A year or two after it had been established on the Dorset Square site, the Cricket Club became known as the Marylebone Cricket Club, merely because it was now based in that parish. A more detailed explanation can be found in my book *The History of Cricket: From The Weald to The World* published by The Stationery Office in 1997.

On 4 July 1835 J.H.Dark had taken over the lease of Lord's Ground and, one suspects, was devising ways of attracting larger crowds to matches. One of the long-standing major Lord's fixtures was Gentlemen v Players, but with the former side so weak, this was hardly a nail-biting contest.

Clarke either declined or was not chosen for the North in the 1837 game, though he had played the previous year. Curiously the North team included Harry Hall, a very obscure player, who was later a groundsman at Trent Bridge. Was he playing in place of Clarke? The other Nottingham players were Garrat, Barker, Jarvis, Redgate and Rothera. Vincent, Marsden and Dearman represented Sheffield. The South won by five wickets due to Lillywhite's bowling – Barker seemingly again did not bowl. A fortnight later Nottinghamshire played Sussex on Brown's Ground. Clarke was absent, even though his name (at the head of the list and therefore most probably captain) was printed in the eleven on 21 July, three days before the game started. John Gibson replaced Clarke. Was this absence from away matches due to illness in the family? It is the most likely explanation.

The Nottinghamshire team had squeezed in an extra match whilst in the South, going direct from Brighton to meet Kent at Town Malling, where Fuller Pilch was installed. This was for the first meeting of the two counties. The team lost to Sussex by three wickets and by nine wickets to Kent.

Before the return with Sussex a practice match, County v Town, was played on The Forest. Clarke hit 43, the only innings over 15 on either side; Butler Parr (no relation of George) of Radcliffe on Trent made 14 not out and was given his place in the county side v Sussex. It was a third defeat – though the report stated 20,000 attended on the second day.

Just over a week later William Clarke's wife Jane died at the age of 39 – she was buried at St Nicholas' Church in Nottingham on 3 September. *The Stamford Mercury* of 8 September 1837 carries the following death notice: 'On the 30th ult, aged 39, Mrs Clarke, wife of Mr W.Clarke, Bell Inn, Market Place, Nottingham.'

On 11 September a match was played 'in a field of Mrs Chapman's at the Trent Bridge' (see *Nottingham Review*) between Holme Lane and Mansfield. Holme Lane had William Clarke as a given man. The latter club overwhelmed Mansfield, scoring 44 and 93 against Mansfield's 24 and 35. Clarke's innings of 20 was the highest in the game – no one on the Mansfield side reached double figures. In the *Nottingham Mercury* the match is described as being 'in a close adjoining Mrs Chapman's Inn at the Trent Bridge'.

On 5 December 1837 William Clarke, widower, innkeeper of Angel Row, Market Place, Nottingham, married Mary Chapman, widow, Trent Bridge Inn, Bridgford. The witnesses were Robert Jackson and Mary Singlehirst [sic]. It was just three months since the death of Clarke's first wife. William Clarke's father was given as John Clark, builder and Mary Chapman was given as daughter of Joseph Singlehirst [sic].

Clarke's new wife was born Mary Ann Singlehurst, and baptised at West Bridgford Parish Church on 30 November 1788, the eldest of the four children of Joseph and Ann Singlehurst (née Horseley). The other three children were Edward (b 1797), Charles (b 1801) and William (b 1805). All three boys have some connection with cricket, their names appearing occasionally in local published matches; for example, when West Bridgford played Mr Samuel Chapman's XI in 1822 William played for West Bridgford, whilst Charles and Edward appear for Mr Chapman's XI.

Mary Ann Singlehurst, then 22, had married Samuel Chapman, a 51-year-old bachelor, in West Bridgford Parish Church on 12 March 1811. In the trade directories of 1799 and 1814, Samuel Chapman is described as a blacksmith of Trent Bridge, but by 1818 he is a victualler and blacksmith of the Horse Shoes, Trent Bridge (or in other versions, the Three Horse Shoes). Samuel Chapman and Mary Ann had two children: these were Samuel Chapman, baptised in West Bridgford, 26 May 1812; and John, baptised in West Bridgford, 4 December 1814. Samuel Chapman was buried in West Bridgford churchyard on 24 November 1825, and the 1832 Trade Directory gives Mary Ann Chapman as living at the Bridge Inn, Trent Bridge, whilst Edward Singlehurst is a blacksmith of West Bridgford and William Singlehurst a farmer of West Bridgford.

On his second marriage Clarke moved to the Trent Bridge Inn. West Bridgford was still a small village – the population in 1801 was 235 and in 1871 had increased by just two more inhabitants. Later, between 1871 and 1891 the village had a dramatic rise, the population increasing tenfold, then by 1914 to 13,000. In 1837 it comprised the Hall, the parish church and a handful of cottages around the church, a few gentlemen's houses and scattered farms, together with the Trent Bridge Inn, formerly the Horse Shoes. The land in the village was owned by the Musters family of Colwick Hall, which stood on the north bank of the River Trent. The first bridge linking West Bridgford with the town of Nottingham was reportedly built in or about 924, but by 1838 the bridge, which had been reconstructed several times, was a multi-arched narrow stone structure: a new bridge was built in 1871 adjacent to the old one, which was demolished the following year.

The following description gives a feel of West Bridgford in Clarke's years there:

> From the Trent Bridge to the little village was nearly half-a-mile, down a narrow lane, with hedges and overhanging trees. The long bridge over the brook on Bridgford Road consisted of seven arches, but wide enough for one vehicle only, guarded by posts and rails. It was an ideal country village, with its embowered church, the squire's hall, two or three gentlemen's houses, each cottage in a garden, with woodbine, honeysuckle, jasmine or roses adorning the front, big trees in the crofts, several farm houses with orchards and the vigorous rippling brook running down from its spring; the cattle grazing in the fields, with tall hedges and quietness everywhere.

The first mention of a cricket match in West Bridgford with Clarke's name attached to the venue, was published in the *Nottingham Review* of Friday, 1 June 1838:

> On Monday [28 May] the match between ten players selected [by Clarke] from Bingham, Ratcliffe [sic] and Holme Lane Clubs against ten of the New Forest Club with Barker, was played in a field adjoining Mr Clarke's Trent Bridge Inn. The following is the score of the day's play, which was however, interrupted by rain in the afternoon; but Clarke's side having so great an advantage, the game was given up in their favour.

The New Forest Club made 60 and 60 for seven; Clarke's side 105. Clarke bowled out four in the first innings and three in the second; he also scored 17 not out. There is a Chapman (no initial) in Clarke's side – presumably John.

In August, when Bingham played Holme Lane on the Trent Bridge ground, the *Nottingham Review* adds a note: 'It is but justice to Mr Clarke to say that he has displayed great judgment in laying out the Trent Bridge Ground and the admirable condition in which it is kept renders it a delightful place for the practice of this healthiest and most manly of British Sports.' (Clarke was flying in the face of the opinion expressed in 1836 that private grounds were a thing to be abhorred because the profits went to the owner and, as the years were to tell, he rued the day he founded Trent Bridge Cricket Ground.)

The match itself was significant in that William Clarke scored 128 of the 248 Holme Lane total, and Bingham were all out for 14 and 15! The *Nottingham Journal* notes: 'Clarke was never in better play than this season: he is becoming the Pilch of the Midland Counties. The Trent Bridge ground is beautifully laid out and is kept in admirable order under the spirited superintendence of Mr Clarke.' In 1837 the road, about three miles in length linking the Trent Bridge Inn to Radcliffe on Trent, was called Gamston Lane as far as the hamlet of Gamston and then Holme Lane for the remainder of its journey. (It is now Radcliffe Road and in part the A52.) The Holme Lane Cricket Club took its name from this road.

Nottingham City Council's plaque on the Bell Inn recognising Clarke's 'judgement' at Trent Bridge.

The first important local match of 1838 was the annual Town v County fixture. This was however played on The Forest. Clarke appeared for the County; also in the County side was John Chapman, his recently acquired younger stepson. This game therefore had not been moved to Clarke's new ground, but on 9 July, a similar match entitled Barker's Side v Clarke's Side took place on Clarke's New Ground at Trent Bridge.

The other notable Nottingham match – no matches were arranged with teams outside the county – was on 3 September on The Forest, Nottingham Old Club First Eleven with A.Mynn and Caldecourt v The Next Twenty-Two of Nottinghamshire. Clarke captained the Twenty-Two, who won by 194 runs. The Eleven were all out for 36 and 49, but only four of their twenty wickets were bowled down, so it is impossible to give any credit to a specific bowler. The highest scorer in the match with 27 was Charles Brown – the report comments: 'This is the first match of importance for Charles Brown since he has not played for or against the Old Club until now.'

During 1838 there were three major matches in the south that involved Nottinghamshire players, but Clarke was not chosen for any of them. No fewer than seven (Barker, Heath, Garrat, Jarvis, Guy, Gibson and Redgate) were in the North XI v South at Lord's. The South won by eight wickets and the next bona fide North v South game was not played until 1849. The Gentlemen v Players game at Lord's saw Barker, Garrat, Jarvis, Guy and Redgate in the professional eleven and finally Guy, Redgate, Jarvis and Garrat played in the England side v Sussex at Brighton – Haygarth notes that it was really Kent and Nottinghamshire v Sussex.

The first match of note played on the Trent Bridge Ground in 1839 was for £20-a-side: this was Thomas Barker and XIII of the Rancliffe Arms Club versus William Clarke and ten of the Town and County. (The Rancliffe Arms was a Nottingham pub which for several years fielded a strong cricket side.) Clarke achieved little, though his side won by a fair margin, the most successful player being Butler Parr whose 'batting and stumping was very much admired'.

The only two matches in Sutton's book for 1839 were two single-wicket contests at Trent Bridge. George Jarvis was beaten by Isaac Johnson of the Rancliffe Arms club; later Isaac Johnson and George Butler (Mansfield) were beaten by Butler Parr and Henry Crook. The *Nottingham Review* of September 13 announced that the annual Town v County match would be played at Trent Bridge the following Monday – the teams are listed, but no report appears; perhaps the game was rained off? However, it indicates that Clarke had wrested this principal local fixture off the Forest Ground.

By 1840 the old Forest Ground was almost completely overshadowed by Clarke's Trent Bridge. He organized three genuine inter-county games, home and away with Sussex and away against Kent. No fewer than five amateurs were included in the Notts team that Clarke took to play Sussex and then immediately afterwards Kent, in June. The letters to the 'Nobility and Gentry' had borne fruit in financing the week's adventures in the south of England, but as a result professionals of greater talent had to be omitted. Sussex won by an innings and 59 runs! The amateurs included T.B.Charlton, son of William Charlton of Chilwell Hall, and Edwin Patchitt, who, at the age of 23, as a clerk to the county magistrates, had the unenviable task of reading the Riot Act proclamation in front of the infuriated mob who burnt down Nottingham Castle. He was a solicitor and in the 1850s was Mayor of Nottingham. T.B.Redgate was also a solicitor, latterly living on a small estate near Weston, Newark (he was no relation

The Trent Bridge Inn, in about 1840, at the time of Nottinghamshire's first inter-county match, against Sussex, on the adjoining cricket ground. Nearly 1,600 first-class matches have now been played there, including 60 Tests.

of Sam Redgate); the other amateurs, Creswell and Foxcroft, have been previously mentioned. In 1841 T.B.Charlton was the principal promoter of the first attempt to set up a formal Nottinghamshire County Cricket Club. One assumes he had noted that Sussex had just founded such a County Club. The main reason for such a club was to finance the cost of county away matches. Charlton's creation however seems to have led a rather shadowy existence, if only because Clarke was such a dominant figure in local Notts cricket and, of course, controlled his newly laid-out Trent Bridge Ground.

Clarke opened the batting for the county, both in the Sussex match and the one v Kent at Town Malling, where Isaac Johnson replaced Patchitt who had to return to Nottingham on business. Notts beat Kent with Clarke taking nine wickets in the second innings and Guy hitting an unbeaten 73 – quite a feat against the bowling of Alfred Mynn and William Hillyer. It was the first time that Clarke had taken nine wickets in an innings in a 'first-class' match. Unfortunately the detailed bowling analysis has never been found, but with both Pilch and Mynn among the opposition batsmen, it is possibly Clarke's greatest bowling feat. It is a surprise, in view of Clarke's brilliant bowling, that he was not chosen for the North of England v MCC at Lord's a month later; even more surprising because the North included Abram Bass (of the Burton brewery family) and G.M.Kettle, two amateurs who were hardly of county standard. (Both played once for Notts in 1843.)

From Clarke's viewpoint the most significant match of the summer was Nottinghamshire v Sussex on 27 and 28 July 1840. It was the first inter-county contest ever staged at Trent Bridge. Clarke opened the batting and performed well in a low-scoring game, hitting 17 and 13. He also took six wickets in Sussex's second innings – Notts seemed certain to win with the score 66 for five and only 38 required, but the last four wickets went down for one run, Nottinghamshire losing by 14. From Clarke's angle the monetary returns were less than expected – the match lasted two days instead of three and the crowds were modest now that spectators had to pay.

Clarke arranged, at Trent Bridge, what for Nottingham was a new fixture: Gentlemen v Players. On 8 June the one innings per side game ended in a tie. The Gentlemen were aided by three professionals. A return match, again at Trent Bridge, was won by the Players by five wickets. Another innovation was the game Gentlemen of Nottinghamshire with Clarke versus Chaddesden and Burton upon Trent with S.Dakin. No doubt this game was organized through Abram Bass. Sam Dakin was a professional with the South Derbyshire Club, but played one game for Nottinghamshire in 1845. Dakin hit an unbeaten 51 to take his side to an eight-wicket victory. Finally on September 11, Nottinghamshire opposed Capt Hogge's XI at Trent Bridge, winning by an innings, with Sam Parr making 72 and Tom Barker 52.

In the spring of 1841 the first detailed census was taken. The address of the Trent Bridge Inn is historically interesting since the Nottingham

Town boundary went through the inn and, according to an old tale, when beating the bounds the locals of West Bridgford had to climb through the windows. (It is only since the Second World War that the boundaries between Nottingham and West Bridgford were regularized and the line made to follow the course of the River Trent.) The inn is given as in London Road, St Mary's District of Nottingham. The persons listed for the inn are: William Clarke, publican, aged 40; Mary Clarke, wife, aged 45; Jane Clarke, daughter, aged 10; Joseph Gillow, servant, aged 30; Edward Diggle, servant, aged 15; Mary Kiddy, servant, aged 20; Elizabeth Radley, servant, aged 15; Richard Robotham, boatman, aged 35; Edward Jilbourne, boatman, aged 25; Thomas James, boatman, aged 60; John Beck, boatman, aged 20. Jane Clarke is William Clarke's daughter by his first wife. Absent is Alfred Clarke who would be aged ten. In the 1841 census there is an Alfred Clarke, aged nine, at the Friends' School, Ackworth, Yorkshire, who is noted as not born in Yorkshire. It is possible this is William Clarke's son.

The Trent Bridge season began early – on 12 April – when fourteen Gentlemen opposed eleven Players. John Foxcroft made the highest score in the match, but most of his fellow gentlemen failed and the Players won, then batted on. Of more interest is the note that the Nottingham Amateur Club, whose president is John Galloway, consists of local tradesmen and their practice ground is Trent Bridge – Clarke presumably received some income from this club's use of the ground. The only inter-county game arranged for Nottinghamshire during the summer was against Kent at Trent Bridge – play rather followed the pattern of the home Sussex match of 1840, Notts' batting falling apart in the second innings when, at 53 for six, 33 were required, but the game was lost by 22 runs. Clarke took five wickets in the first innings, though he failed with the bat – one and nought; he still put himself down as an opener or at No.3.

There were two MCC v North matches. In the first, at Lord's, Notts had six representatives, but not Clarke, in the Northern eleven and won by 66 runs. The return game, no doubt due to Abram Bass, was played at Burton upon Trent. William Clarke opened the batting. Redgate was selected but after an over or two retired – one suspects due to drink. Bass batted for him. Due to the batting of Billy Good, who made 82, the North lost by an innings.

The advertised North eleven for the Lord's fixture the following season, listed in the *Nottingham Review* of 17 June 1842, read: T.B.Charlton, C.Creswell, F.Noyes, E.Patchitt, J.Foxcroft, T.Barker, W.Clarke, S.Redgate, J.Oscroft, J.Guy and either C.Brown or G.Butler. All twelve were Nottinghamshire players. However: when the match began the following Monday, six of the players in the above list, including Clarke, were missing. The *Nottingham Review* simply states 'Several Notts men were dropped from the North team, for an unknown reason.'

Clarke was not amused and on 1 July there was an announcement: 'Mr Clarke with a Nottinghamshire Eleven, challenges MCC for money or just for a game, because Nottinghamshire players had been dropped from the North team last week.' MCC rose to the challenge and the game took place

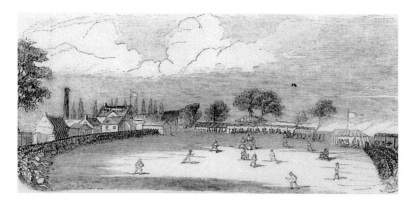

*The Trent Bridge ground, under a Constable-style cloudscape,
showing the match between Nottinghamshire and England under way
in August 1842; the visitors won.*

Trent Bridge Cricket Ground
NOTTINGHAM.

All England AGST. Nottingham,
For 100 Sovereigns.
Monday, Tuesday, and Wednesday, Aug. 22, 23, & 24, 1842
Umpires—Messrs. Bailey and Caldecourt, of the Mary-le-bone Ground.

Statement of the Game, from the Scorers' List :—

ALL ENGLAND.
FIRST INNINGS.

Lillywhite, b Barker	3
Hillyer, c Noyes (b Clarke)	0
Box, b Redgate	11
Pilch, b Redgate	60
Mr. A. Mynn, b Clarke	61
Wenman, st Guy (b Clarke)	21
Sewell, st Guy (b Clarke)	33
Hon. F. Ponsonby, c B. Parr (b Clarke)	7
Hawkins, c Clarke (b Clarke)	12
Dorrington, not out	0
Dean, c Noyes (b Clarke)	7
Byes	2
Wide balls	4
No balls	7
	228

NOTTINGHAM.
FIRST INNINGS.

B. Parr, c Pilch (b Mynn)	6
Clarke, b Hillyer	18
Barker, c Ponsonby (b Hillyer)	17
Guy, c Box (b Mynn)	8
S. Parr, b Lillywhite	15
Mr. Noyes, b Dean	12
Butler, c Ponsonby (b Dean)	12
Good, c Lillywhite (b Dean)	3
Oscroft, run out	6
Mr. Chapman, b Mynn	11
Redgate, not out	8
Byes	4
Wide balls	2
	122

NOTTINGHAM.
SECOND INNINGS.

Redgate, b Mynn	8
Mr. Noyes, c Hillyer (b Mynn)	6
Oscroft, b Lillywhite	4
Guy, b Mynn	3
Barker, c Dorrington (b Lillywhite)	3
S. Parr, b Mynn	5
Butler, c Ponsonby (b Hillyer)	21
B. Parr, c Wenman (b Lillywhite)	0
Clarke, b Mynn	28
Good, c Pilch (b Mynn)	15
Mr. Chapman, not out	1
Byes, 6 ; wide, 3	9
	110

ALL ENGLAND.
SECOND INNINGS.

Dorrington, not out	3
Dean, not out	1
Bye	1
	5

ROBERT HICKLING, PRINTER, NOTTINGHAM.

*Scorecard of the match usually styled nowadays as Nottinghamshire v England,
played at Trent Bridge in August 1842. Despite Clarke's seven for 98
in England's first innings the visitors won by ten wickets.*

at Trent Bridge beginning on 22 August under the title Nottinghamshire v England, the latter team being raised by Fuller Pilch rather than MCC. Clarke had an outstanding all-round match. He made the highest score in both Nottinghamshire innings, though admittedly only 18 and 26, but also took seven of England's ten wickets. He was out-gunned by Alfred Mynn, however, whose all-round performance saw him hit 61 and take, in all, nine wickets: Pilch himself scored 60 and his team won by ten wickets. It must have been a chastening experience for Clarke especially as the game was for £100-a-side. The *Nottingham Date Book* however notes: 'The All England Eleven is probably the most formidable that our players have ever contended with.' John Chapman, Clarke's stepson, made his county debut in this game, as did Francis Noyes.

Clarke organized home and away games with the Sheffield Wednesday club, both ending in convincing victories for Nottingham. At Sheffield, the report notes 'Clarke's slow yet sure style did great execution.' The crowds were still not being attracted to Trent Bridge in great numbers. When the Sherwood Forest Club opposed Southwell on The Forest the reported attendance for the first day was 3,000. The following week Clarke staged at Trent Bridge a game Six Gentlemen of Notts with Five Players of England v Nottinghamshire, but only 600 watched the first day's play. Clarke himself did well, opening the batting and being last man out for 75 out of 155: this was his highest innings in first-class matches.

Clarke's efforts to make the Trent Bridge a paying proposition resulted in an 1843 expansion of major match fixtures on the ground. England in general was coming out of recession and maybe Clarke saw more money in people's pockets. The increase sounds modest by present-day standards, but in comparison with the five previous seasons it was a considerable improvement. The Nottingham/Nottinghamshire side had staged no matches there in 1838, one in 1839, two in 1840, one in 1841, three in 1842. In 1843, there was a three-day match in May against Sheffield, in June the first-ever Notts game with Hampshire, in August against MCC and in September against Sussex. In addition to these there were away matches. Clarke opened the season in mid-April with the regular County v Town match – the *Nottingham Review* comments: 'A young bowler named Grundy of Carrington engaged annually by the Sherwood Forest Club gave an excellent specimen of skill, lowering Guy with an exceedingly fine ball.'

James Grundy would develop into a great all-rounder for Nottinghamshire and play an important role in Clarke's career latterly. There were two Gentlemen v Players matches at Trent Bridge in August and September. A new team called Professional Gentlemen used Trent Bridge for two published matches. In cricket terms the team's title might cause some head scratching, but a note after the first game adds 'the professional gentlemen being members of the legal and medical professions'. John Chapman is in the side presumably because he was studying to be a vet. The Notts Amateurs Club in 1843 is given as the 'Amateur Club of Trent Bridge' when it plays an away match at Southwell. Clarke played in all the Nottinghamshire matches of the year.

Thomas Chamberlayne, better known in yachting circles and a large landowner in Hampshire, was making an attempt to revive the cricketing fortunes of his county. He was responsible for financing the Hampshire side to Trent Bridge, which side played a match at Lord's before travelling north. Hampshire's game with MCC was a close-fought affair, though principally due to the talents of Fenner, the Cambridge professional. At Trent Bridge, Redgate, Barker and Clarke were too much for Hampshire – they lost by an innings. The return contest at Day's Ground remains memorable as the only 'major' county contest in which a batsman was allowed to bat twice in each innings. Francis Noyes was permitted to have his innings and then bat again in place of Thomas Barker, whose leg, as we noted earlier, had been broken when he leapt from a runaway hansom cab crossing London to change trains. Nottinghamshire included the Rev Henry Maltby in their eleven. A later brief notice on Maltby states: 'He was a feeble bat and poor bowler, and rumour has it that he was indebted to a *douceur* to old Clarke for his appearances for the County.' Abram Bass also played, presumably to defray expenses, and Notts won by 39 runs. On the return from Southampton, Nottinghamshire played MCC at Lord's – Notts included E.S.E.Hartopp, a member of MCC, in their team, probably on the grounds that his father was the incumbent at West Leake. Sussex were only played once, on 18, 19 and 20 September, at Trent Bridge. Ten days prior to the match taking place, the press reported: 'For the Benefit of Clarke – Mr F.Noyes is the Treasurer of the Committee formed to organize the game.' This therefore was the first Nottinghamshire inter-county match staged for a player's benefit. The report on the match itself notes that Butler Parr and Sam Parr declined to play, John Chapman and John Gilbert taking their places. Gilbert hit 91 which stood for 16 years as the highest individual innings for Notts – he was never to approach this total again in county games. Clarke took twelve Sussex wickets and victory was by an innings. I was unable to find a report on the financial returns to Clarke of the match.

Denison's 1844 *Cricketer's Companion* publishes averages for 1843 after the match scores. Clarke finishes eighth in the 'Batters' list with 11 innings and 170 runs and top of the 'Slow Bowlers' list with 36 wickets, average 5 and 1/7 per match. Denison includes the two Sheffield matches in his statistics, even though his match scores section omits not only the Sheffield game at Trent Bridge, but also the Trent Bridge game v Hampshire. Judged by Denison's figures, the only all-rounder with better statistics than Clarke in 1843 was Alfred Mynn. Clarke was not chosen for 'England' in the five important matches played under that title (mainly England selected by MCC) or for the Gentlemen v Players match at Lord's, which, based on Denison's figures, would appear rather remiss of MCC. It is important to consider Denison's statistics, rather than those compiled later using a different set of matches – the cricket followers of 1843 would obviously judge the merits of players by the figures published at the time.

Not a single Nottinghamshire match was organized by Clarke in 1844. Denison's *Cricketer's Companion* covering the 1844 season includes the following passage, written in April 1845, in the author's review of the season:

> ... and at Northampton, where the first 'Grand Match' witnessed in that locality was played last August, great efforts are being made with a view of constituting such a club as shall be worthy of that sporting and spirited district; whilst Nottingham long famous for its Cricketers, although somewhat slow in its movements in 1844, has already promulgated a promise to be often in the field in 1845. It was a source of disappointment last year that the great talent of which Nottingham and its vicinity can boast was so seldom placed before the public.

I have been unable to find in local newspapers, or the various books on county cricket, any reason for Clarke's decision not to arrange matches, though perhaps the financial returns for 1843 were not as rosy as Clarke anticipated. The only difference in the Nottingham cricket scene in 1844 compared with earlier years is the creation of the Nottinghamshire County Club at Southwell. This all-amateur side, which played originally under the title 'Nottinghamshire', was later to play as 'Gentlemen of Nottinghamshire'. Their first extant match score, v Grantham on 8 and 9 July 1844, has five of the eleven – C.Batchelor, F.Noyes, T.B.Redgate, C.Creswell and J.B.Warwick – who represented the full Nottinghamshire side on occasion. In this initial game they beat Grantham by an innings and 43 runs. Maybe the foundation of this club caused a temporary jolt to Clarke's plans for more county games at Trent Bridge. The nearest Trent Bridge came to a quality match in 1844 was the hybrid Gents of Notts with four Players of England v Players of Notts. This took place during the second week of September and the feature in it picked up by the press was: 'George Parr's batting was superior to anything we have seen for some time.' Parr, a younger brother of Sam Parr, had been born in Radcliffe on Trent in 1826 and was therefore aged 18. It was his first appearance in a match of this quality; he was destined to succeed Fuller Pilch as England's premier batsman and to act as Clarke's lieutenant, and then to take over control of the All-England Eleven and Nottinghamshire on the death of the latter.

William Clarke played in the two North v MCC matches of 1844 and also for England v Kent at Canterbury. Whilst bowling in the Canterbury match, Clarke achieved a hat-trick spread over the two Kent innings and most unusually the hat-trick involved dismissing the same player twice, J.F.Fagge, who batted at No.11 in the first innings and then came in at No.3 when Kent lost their first wicket in the first over. Clarke took twenty-four wickets in these three games, plus seven in the Gents of Notts v Players of Notts at Trent Bridge. Denison's averages give him 34 wickets and add another match to his record, which has me baffled, but it's not a major problem! His name appears in only four 'local' matches published in the *Nottingham Review,* two for Holme Lane, one for Junior Forest Club and one for the minor Gentlemen v Players match at Trent Bridge on 19 August.

The 1845 season is infamous for the recording that Clarke claimed all ten wickets in an innings playing for Nottinghamshire v Leicestershire. The match was played at Trent Bridge on 16 and 17 June. Denison styles it as 'Nottinghamshire v Leicestershire'. Haygarth in *Scores and Biographies* opts for Leicester County Club v Nottinghamshire County Club, but the *Nottingham Review*, advertising the Nottingham team on 6 June, describes the team as Nottingham Amateur Eleven with Clarke against Leicestershire. The names certainly confirm that the team is the Nottingham Amateur Club based at Trent Bridge. Be that as it may, the detailed score in the newspaper, as well as in Denison and Haygarth, credits Clarke with nine wickets with the tenth lbw by an unnamed bowler. The idea that the game was 'first-class' and that Clarke took all ten appears to have been invented by Ashley-Cooper in his Cricket Records section in *Wisden*. (The feat first appeared in the 1902 *Wisden*, which was the first year Ashley-Cooper assisted with statistics in general, and last appeared in the 1963 edition, when it was removed following comments made by Rowland Bowen and Keith Warsop.) Clarke also played in the return match at Leicester, when the Nottingham Amateur side lost by an innings.

However in the bona fide Notts v Kent game at Trent Bridge Clarke returned figures of 27-11-29-9 and 29-8-40-7, his best match return in 'first-class' matches, and in the first fixture at Canterbury he had captured six wickets in the only innings of Kent.

It was during these two matches when the well-known tale involving Felix and Clarke was told. Felix scored 54 at Canterbury and when going in to bat at Trent Bridge was encouraged with cries of, 'Here comes Clarke's master!' Felix clearly entered into the spirit of the event and reportedly took his guard four yards in front of the wicket. The scoresheet reads 'b Clarke 0'. The master bowler had his revenge! When Clarke played for England against Kent at Canterbury, he took 12 wickets in the match. It had been altogether an outstanding season for him.

The final fixture he arranged for 1845 at Trent Bridge was Fourteen of Notts v England: Denison comments:

A match now-a-days of an unusual character was played at Nottingham in the early part of September, 'Eleven of England v Fourteen of Nottingham'. From a variety of circumstances, the former were unable to gather their strength, for they went into the field without either Mr Felix, Mr A.Mynn, or Mr C.Taylor. The match was stated to have been made by a gentleman at Manchester, and most probably that was so. At all events it did not owe its origins to the Marylebone Club, of whose members it was much to be regretted so few made their appearance at Nottingham, even as spectators. The fight between the contending parties was severe and led to some of the most brilliant play of the season. Towards the latter part of the match on the Saturday, the third day, the interest became very intense, especially with the many who had sported large sums in the shape of bets upon it. This will readily be conceived when it is stated that an hour before its termination the betting was free at 5 and 6 to 1 against Nottingham, whilst they eventually became conquerors by six wickets.

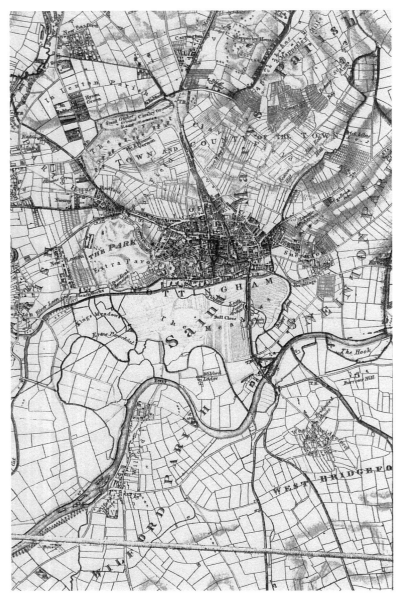

Nottingham in 1836, with the overcrowded town surrounded by open fields.
Trent Bridge and its Inn are about a mile south-east of the built-up area.
The Forest cricket ground, Trent Bridge's early rival,
is near the top of the map.

Clarke, when about to bowl, ran out Royston who was backing up, which greatly amused the crowd. The match was, in terms of its result, a suitable finale to Clarke's occupation of the Trent Bridge Inn and its adjoining cricket ground, although there is no indication in the contemporary press that this was to be the case.

Chapter Seven
Leaving Trent Bridge

On 20 March 1846 the following notice appeared in the *Nottingham Review*: 'Mr W.Clark, the celebrated slow bowler, is removing from Nottingham and will in future be found on Lord's Ground.'

Over the past years, historians, myself included, have given the impression that Clarke, unable to obtain a financial return from laying out Trent Bridge Cricket Ground, conceived the idea of creating a team of notable players to tour up and down England. In order to put this scheme into practice he moved to London, where he could negotiate terms with suitable players and arrange fixtures. Ashley-Cooper in his long essay on Clarke, see *Nottinghamshire Cricket and Cricketers*, page 41, states: 'The [Trent Bridge] Inn remained Clarke's home until 1847, when he retired from business and decided to devote all his attention to cricket.' This remark comes straight from Sutton's *Nottinghamshire Cricket Matches from 1771 to 1853*, published in 1853, *viz*: 'Clark retired from business as an innkeeper in 1847 and devoted himself to his favourite game.'

If Clarke had moved to Lord's in 1846, as the newspaper states, but kept the Trent Bridge Inn as his home and business until 1847, one would have thought that he would have played the occasional match on the Trent Bridge Ground in the 1846 season, but his name does not appear in a single game in Nottingham that summer. A further newspaper report in the *Morning Post* of 21 April 1846 removes any lingering doubts about Clarke leaving Nottingham: 'On Saturday morning [18 April]....an attempt was made to set fire to premises belonging to Mr Chapman, landlord of the Trent Bridge Inn. ... This is the second attempt in twenty-one days to fire the same premises.' (The fire was in a barn/stables, filled with hay, about 30 yards from the Inn itself.)

Twenty or more years ago, the Singlehurst family, whose main branch had been based in West Bridgford, produced the most elaborate family tree, but one of the few gaps was the 'disappearance' of Mary Singlehurst, who became Mary Chapman, then in 1837 Mary Clarke. The question arises, 'Did she move to London with William Clarke in 1846?' Both William and Mary Clark(e) being such common names it proved too difficult to locate her in London and the surrounding area.

In the 1851 census, however, she is living with her son, John Chapman, at his house in Gainsborough. Nothing remarkable about that, except that she is described as a 'widow', which could fool very few, since her husband's name was constantly in the newspapers. It cannot be a coincidence that in 1851, when Clarke's All-England Eleven played no fewer than 34 three-day matches during the season, the only one from which Clarke is absent is the game at Gainsborough on 26, 27 and 28 May. He played in the matches immediately before and after. John Chapman opened the batting for Gainsborough. Later in her life, Mary Clarke occasionally switched her name back to Mary Chapman.

The conclusion I have drawn from these facts is that William Clarke's marriage broke up and he had little option but to move out of the Trent Bridge Inn and Nottingham. John Chapman, who had married and moved away from the Trent Bridge Inn before 1841, returned to the Inn as soon as Clarke left (as is shown by the notice regarding the Trent Bridge Inn fire), and for three seasons ran the Inn and Cricket Ground and then moved in 1849 to Gainsborough where he set up business as a vet. He was to live in Gainsborough for the rest of his life.

Clarke joined the Lord's staff of 'ground bowlers', as they were termed, in 1846, which itself is difficult to understand. He was aged 47. It is most unfortunate (from the historians' viewpoint) that Denison's book *Sketches of the Players* was written in May 1846. It includes a long biography of Clarke. Denison's essay ends with Clarke's statistics for 1845, which credit him with 106 wickets at more than eight per match, plus as a batsman 261 runs, average 12.5, making him one of the outstanding all-rounders, but the book is published too early to mention Clarke's 1846 career move.

An overcrowded Lord's ground in 1842. Clarke joined the MCC bowling staff here in 1846, eventually playing fifty first-class matches at the ground; among other tasks, he umpired the Eton v Harrow match of 1847.

James Dark had taken over the lease of Lord's Cricket Ground in 1835, as previously mentioned, and by the time Clarke arrived there, Dark had eight men and six boys employed 'under his general superintendence'. I assume that Clarke was acquainted with Dark and filled a vacancy as one of the bowlers – the boys were described as 'scouts'. Clarke's first recorded match of 1846 was a curious affair, the Oxford University players splitting themselves into those from the North and those from the South, then the two resulting teams being reinforced by several professionals. Clarke played for the North and took eight of the ten wickets in the South's only innings – the North batsmen failed miserably twice before Hillyer and Dean. His first recorded game at Lord's in 1846 was played in honour of N.Felix, the match title being Pilch's XI v Felix's XI. Clarke was in Felix's team, taking just three wickets in a low-scoring match. North v MCC at Lord's was another low-scoring affair, Clarke took ten wickets for the North. For England v Kent at Lord's, Clarke obtained five wickets in the first innings, but wasn't required in the second, when Lillywhite and Dean bowled Kent out for 66. Being on the Lord's staff meant that Clarke was picked for Players v Gentlemen, his debut in this series.

His first match actually for MCC as such, was not until 27 and 28 July when he played against Norfolk – the wickets of the county were shared, with Lillywhite taking 11, Clarke six , Hillyer three. He went to Canterbury, being part of the England eleven (picked by MCC) to play Kent, and again took a number of wickets and afterwards travelled on to Brighton for the England match v Sussex – Clarke opened the batting in both these England matches. That game saw the end of his MCC involvement for 1846.

On 27 and 28 August a match was played for Clarke's benefit at Southwell. It was entitled Five Gentlemen of the Southwell Club and Five Players of Nottinghamshire with Mynn v England. This was the match when George Parr seemingly rowed from Radcliffe to Southwell along the Trent and underestimated the time it would take – he arrived late. Clarke was exceedingly angry and despite Parr scoring 51, the highest for the local team, Clarke omitted him from the three ground-breaking All-England Eleven matches arranged for the following fortnight. Haygarth in *Scores and Biographies* states Parr was taken ill and unable to play: in a third version, Parr left Southwell before the match ended – whether or not by boat is not stated! The Southwell game seems to have been a 'warm-up' fixture prior to the first England matches – ten of the eleven in the first England game played in the match at Southwell. The first All-England Eleven match took place v XVIII of Sheffield at Hyde Park on 31 August and the two following days. The games at Manchester and Leeds came directly afterwards. The way in which Clarke was going, knowingly or unknowingly, to change cricket's history, was just beginning.

From the 1780s, the Cricket Club which became known as Marylebone Cricket Club when it established itself at the first of Thomas Lord's grounds, effectively, though perhaps not deliberately, took control of cricket. The Cricket Club became the game's equivalent of The Jockey Club, which organization had been formed at the same venue in Pall Mall. The Cricket Club, soon described as MCC, assumed control of the Laws of the game and, due to their income from subscriptions, employed a staff of professional cricketers, which by the 1840s, as noted, numbered 12. F.S.Ashley-Cooper's book on the MCC states that in 1835, the Club had in membership one Duke, two Marquesses, eleven Earls, eight Baronets and 23 Honourables. When Clarke arrived as a professional in 1846, the total MCC membership was 494. The three major inter-public schools matches, as well as the University match, were played on Lord's Ground, which meant that many of the participants in those games became MCC members, and thus the prestige of the Club was maintained and enhanced. The principal cricket fixtures of the 1840s were the Gentlemen v Players matches. In reality, as is illustrated by the fact that Clarke was not invited to participate until 1846, the majority of those taking part were either MCC members or professionals engaged on the ground, so the two teams did not necessarily contain all the best available talent. Any member of the public who wished to watch the best players of the time in anything other than the very occasional match, needed to visit Lord's.

Denison's *Cricketers' Companion* covering the season of 1846 proves just how dominant MCC and Lord's were in cricketing terms. His review of the season devotes some 14 pages to MCC and Lord's-based matches and just a single page to 'other cricket clubs' (*i.e.* the rest of the British Isles).

By the very creation of the All-England Eleven, with its star players and the publicity gained through touring England and later Scotland, Clarke broke the MCC stranglehold on *pukka* cricket and made the sport a truly national game. Clarke enabled the general public to see the great players of the time and a lucky few in each locality – usually twenty-two young hopefuls – could actually test their cricketing ability against England's best. Local newspapers gave extensive coverage to these All-England matches, so even those who were unable to see the cricket itself could read about it.

How and why was Clarke inspired to create this cricketing innovation? Professor West's book *The Elevens of England* is the major work on the subject of Clarke's team and the later teams set up as rivals, but in discussing Clarke's initial concept Professor West states only that Clarke's scheme 'had matured in the same year' (in which he came to Lord's). However, looking at the broader picture, the economy had grown rapidly in the previous four years, with industry doing particularly well. Of course Clarke would not have had any detailed figures and the statistics for the 1840s which are in circulation at the present time have been retrospectively estimated. But he would have known that business confidence, especially in industrial towns, was high and signs were propitious. (As it happens, from 1848 to 1852 the UK economy went into recession, although industry was less adversely affected than other sectors.) Having been a publican for over 25 years, Clarke would have been only too aware of the ebb and flow in sales, as well as the success or otherwise of 'leisure events' staged by his fellow publicans.

There seem to be no extant letters or other manuscript documents that might throw light on how Clarke thought up and organized his brainchild. The first reference to the All-England Eleven in the newspapers seems to be in July 1846 in the Sheffield press, announcing that the match in Sheffield would begin on 31 August. I am of the opinion that Clarke decided on testing out his scheme as a result of the success of the match between England and XIV of Nottinghamshire played at Trent Bridge in September

1845. As has been mentioned, Denison writes, 'The Match was stated to have been made by a gentleman at Manchester.' Who was this man? Is it a pure coincidence that the second All-England match was played on the ground of Manchester Cricket Club?

One of the major amateur supporters of that Club was John Earle. Earle must have been known to Clarke, since both of them played in the Nottingham v Leicester matches through the 1820s, and Earle was a member of the Barrow Club in the north of Leicestershire. Earle left Leicestershire for Manchester where he set himself up in the cotton trade and seems to have flourished. His son, John Henry Earle, was also a keen cricketer and both father and son played for the Manchester team v All-England in September 1846. A search of any archive material relating to Earle and cricket has drawn a blank, so this idea remains just a theory.

Moving to the fortnight before the AEE v Sheffield game of 1846, it is instructive to check the appearances of Clarke's eleven men in the four three-day match sessions in early August 1846, to dispel the impression that the most talented cricketers jumped at Clarke's invitation to join his team because the top players had very few opportunities to earn money from the game. Alfred Mynn and William Hillyer appeared in all four sessions, whilst Dean, Sewell, Guy and Clarke appeared in three of the four. Pilch, Martingell and Butler played in two; though Dorrinton and V.S.C.Smith made just a single appearance. Adding the three England matches, Mynn and Hillyer played in seven successive matches in the three-and-a-half-week period, beginning with the England v Sussex match on 17 August. Ten of the eleven travelled from Southwell up to Sheffield for 31 August. The odd man out was Dorrinton, who had not played since the England v Sussex match at Brighton finishing on 19 August.

The Sheffield and Rotherham Independent, in its long and detailed report on the AEE v Sheffield match, begins by explaining that Mr Felix was absent from the England team due to business, and was replaced by Mr Smith. Butler played for Parr, the latter confined to his bed by illness, or in navigational disgrace, depending on which report one believes. The England team was unchanged for the three matches, though on 29 August the *Leeds Times* advertised only eight of the actual eleven for the Leeds game, with the names of Felix, Parr, T.Box and F.W.Lillywhite making up the squad. On the suitability of the eleven men to claim that they were equal to any contemporary 'picked' eleven and Clarke's judgement of their talents, the following brief notes provide, I feel, the necessary data:

> Alfred Mynn was the star attraction. William Caffyn notes in his reminiscences: 'Mr Mynn was without doubt the most popular cricketer of his day. When I played with him towards the end of his career, he was always the centre of attraction on every cricket field, and the spectators would crowd about him when he walked round the ground like flies round a honey-pot. His immense popularity threw even the superior abilities of Pilch and Parr into the shade. He was beloved by all sorts and conditions of men and he, in return, seemed to think kindly of every one.'

Caffyn skirts round the fact that Mynn was at one time bankrupt, as well as having been in prison for debt. By 1846 his all-round expertise as a fast bowler and hurricane hitter was in decline, but Clarke's decision was a wise move. Mynn was bowled sparingly in All-England matches and, though he often created excitement by hitting boundaries, his occupation of the crease was sadly sometimes brief. Clarke however was happy to have his presence in the squad, because of his drawing powers, even if towards the end, Mynn merely officiated as the team's umpire. Nominally Mynn was an amateur; indeed he represented Gentlemen v Players at Lord's from 1832 to 1852. He had been born at Goudhurst in 1807 and was therefore 39 at the time of the Sheffield match: from 1834 to 1859 he appeared in representative matches for his native Kent. He died at Southwark in 1861.

Villiers Shallet Chernocke Smith was the other amateur in Clarke's side, standing in for the absent Felix. Educated at Winchester College, he was born at Plymouth in 1821 and was in the school XI for five years to 1843 when he was nearly 22. He went up to Oxford University, playing against Cambridge at Lord's for four years, being captain in 1846 and 1847. He was the highest scorer for Oxford in the 1846 match. On ordination he retired from major cricket and did not play for a county side. Smith died in 1871.

Fuller Pilch was the outstanding batsman of his era. Haygarth considered him the best he had seen: 'His style of batting was very commanding, extremely forward and he seemed to crush the best bowling by his long forward plunge before it had time to shoot, or rise, or do mischief by catches.' Caffyn agrees, though he adds: 'Pilch was exceedingly good tempered, and very kind to all young players with whom he came in contact. He was a remarkably quiet man, with no conversation and seemed never happier than when behind a churchwarden pipe, all by himself.' Born in Norfolk in 1804, he was paid to move to Kent in the mid-1830s and played for the latter county from 1836 to 1854. From 1827 to 1849 he appeared for Players v Gentlemen at Lord's. Pilch died in Canterbury in 1870. (The ACS published a biography of Fuller Pilch, by Brian Rendell, in this series in 2010.)

Joseph Guy is described by Richard Daft as 'after Pilch perhaps the most stylish batsman of his day.' He, it was reported, sacrificed runs for the sake of his style and didn't attack the bowling with the skill of Pilch. However, he was chosen for the Players v Gentlemen from 1838 to 1852, which demonstrates the MCC's opinion of his skill. Born in Nottingham in 1813, he played for his native county from 1837 to 1854 and died in 1873.

William Hillyer was called the best of all bowlers and certainly in the mid-1840s he had no equal as a medium-fast round-arm performer; he was the leading wicket-taker in first-class cricket in seven consecutive seasons from 1842 to 1848. Caffyn is full of praise: 'A splendid bowler was the famous Billy Hillyer of the Kent eleven, being one of the very best of the early round-arm bowlers. He bowled medium pace and had a big break from the leg. He obtained many wickets in the slips by bowling on, or just outside the off stumps, and making the ball go away. I used to find him terribly difficult, as his ball went off the pitch so quickly and one was very often too late for him when trying to cut near the wicket, as I generally used to do.' Born at Leybourne, Kent in 1813, he played for Kent from 1835 to 1853 and for the Players from 1838 to 1851; he died at Maidstone in 1861.

William Martingell played for the Players v Gentlemen at Lord's from 1844 to 1858 – Fred Lillywhite in 1857 comments: 'One among the best bowlers of the day; not only pretty often on the spot, but is clever in "dodging" or giving a ball the most difficult to play by his opponent. A steady bat.' Caffyn is slightly critical: 'An excellent fast-medium bowler, though he used, I thought, to allow rather too much for his leg-break, and was often a good deal punished by such players as George Parr in consequence. He was also a very decent bat against fast bowling, but generally too eager to hit when playing against slow.' Martingell was engaged to play for Kent in the days before Surrey had a team, but latterly played for Surrey, being born in the county in 1818. He was a notable coach, being engaged at various times at Rugby, Eton and Bradfield. He died in 1897.

Tom Sewell came from Mitcham, being born there in 1806. His county cricket was limited to a handful of games for Middlesex, Surrey and Kent, but he was on the groundstaff at Lord's and most of his major matches were for MCC, or for matches arranged by the Club. Apart from Clarke himself, he was the oldest of the original AEE team and his time with Clarke's team ended in 1848. He was a useful bat and bowled under-arm. In his later years he was a well-known and reliable umpire. His son Tom Sewell junior, played with success for Kent and Surrey. Sewell senior died in 1888.

James 'Jemmy' Dean is lauded by Fred Lillywhite: 'A very careful bat, and has a strong defence. As a bowler few can surpass him, and in the field you can scarcely put him out of his place. These abilities possessed by an individual are a sufficient proof that no match ought to be played without

Clarke recruited Alfred Mynn, William Hillyer and James Dean, big names all, for his first forays with the All-England Eleven at the end of the 1846 season.

him.' Caffyn describes Dean as the finest long stop in England and noted as a fast bowler but continues: 'He was a little man and very stout in his latter days. He had a queer shambling kind of walk and indeed his appearance altogether was as unlike one's idea of a cricketer as could well be imagined.' Dean was born at Duncton in 1816; he represented Sussex from 1835 to 1860 and the Players v the Gentlemen from 1843 to 1857, but played for the All-England Eleven only until 1849. He died in 1881.

William Dorrinton was born at West Malling in Kent in 1809 and died in November 1848; the cause, according to Haygarth, was a cold caught whilst travelling with the AEE. He played 23 matches for Clarke's side and was considered an excellent wicketkeeper and useful batsman. Unfortunately his career coincided with those of Box and Wenman thus restricting his opportunities as a keeper. He played for Kent from 1836 to 1848 and occasionally for Players v Gentlemen.

George Butler, a useful batsman, who was born in Mansfield in 1810, played for Nottinghamshire from 1841 to 1852, but in only five AEE matches, all three 1846 games and once each in 1847 and 1848. As noted, he only played due to Parr's absence. Latterly he was an umpire and then groundsman at Trent Bridge, dying in Nottingham in 1887.

The above notes on the players have been taken deliberately from contemporary sources, principally Caffyn, Denison and Fred Lillywhite, in order that the reader can obtain a feel for the abilities of the players as felt by those who either played with them, or watched them on a regular basis.

The first three-day All-England Eleven match was arranged for Monday, Tuesday and Wednesday, (31 August, 1 and 2 September 1846) versus XX of Sheffield. The report in the *Sheffield and Rotherham Independent* states:
> This important and interesting match was played ... before the largest number of spectators, we believe, that ever assembled to witness a match since the making of the ground. From the well-known ability of the All England eleven, the names of whom had been for some weeks before the public, the interest excited, not only in the town and its immediate vicinity, but also amongst the lovers of this noble and manly amusement living at a considerable distance, was unusually intense. Parties in vehicles of every description, and groups of pedestrians, thronged our streets early during the mornings of the three days and hundreds availed themselves of the advantages of railway accommodation.

Between five and six thousand people attended each day – one source gives a total of 16,000 in all. Sheffield won the toss, putting the England side in to bat. William Clarke and James Dean opened the batting. Clarke faced the first over, which is succinctly reported: 'The first three balls were played by Clarke without a run, but the last caused a rattle behind.' England were all out for 80 and rain ended the first day's play after Sheffield had faced just three overs without loss. By the close of the second day Sheffield were all out for 72 and England were 85 for six in their second innings. The report notes England were now favourites at considerable odds. On the last day England were all out for 106 and Sheffield then scored the 115 runs for victory having lost 14 wickets. The report concludes: '... which finished one of the most splendid, exciting and important matches that ever was played in this part of the kingdom.' In fact the winning run was an overthrow!

Clarke, despite his first-over duck and the fact that he himself only bowled seven overs, taking a single wicket, must have been delighted with the public interest in his pioneering venture. The England team left Sheffield by train for Manchester, where their match against the town club was due to start the following morning. The venue was the cricket ground in Moss Lane, Hulme. In Sheffield the local club had fielded 20 players, but Manchester decided on 18 which was wildly optimistic, and All-England won by an innings and 31 runs. Fuller Pilch scored 62 of England's 228 runs. Hillyer, Mynn and Dean shared all but two of Manchester's wickets, with Clarke not choosing to bowl himself. As at Sheffield large crowds attended the match and the Manchester Club added to the attraction by engaging the band of the 69th Regiment of Infantry, though Clarke objected to the band playing whilst the match was taking place, so there was music at the dinner interval and close of play. According to the report, the Manchester Club paid all the travelling and other expenses of the visitors totalling about £70.

The England team travelled over the weekend to Leeds, where they opposed Eighteen of Yorkshire on the Victoria Ground at Woodhouse Moor, Leeds, beginning on Monday, 7 September 1846. The ground had been set out in 1837, but this game is described as the first major match staged at the venue. About 3,000 spectators attended on each day. The Yorkshire team was picked from 18 players within 25 miles of Leeds and did not include the Sheffield cricketers. Admission to the ground was one shilling each day or two shillings for all three days. Ladies were admitted free of charge. All-England won by 69 runs; again Clarke did not bowl, Hillyer, Dean and Mynn taking all the wickets. The bowling of J.R.Ibbetson caused much controversy. He was no-balled for illegal deliveries 16 times and the upset was calmed only when the umpires were changed. Despite some unseasonal weather the attendances matched those in Manchester.

The series of three matches having ended, the England Eleven had a final meal at the Haunch of Venison Inn in Leeds, during which the rest of the team presented V.S.C.Smith with a silver-mounted cigar case as a testimonial to his play during the matches. The case was engraved: 'Presented to V.C.Smith, Esq, by the following ten players of England, as a trifling acknowledgment of his valuable aid in the great matches in the north, Sept 8, 1846 – A.Mynn Esq., G.Butler, W.Clark, J.Dean, W.Dorrinton, J.Guy, W.Hillyer, W.Martingell, F.Pilch, T.Sewell.'

The day the Leeds match ended, Clarke, Hillyer, Dean and Pilch travelled to Swaffham, the first three to represent MCC, and Pilch to appear in the opposing Norfolk team. Hillyer and Dean captured all the Norfolk wickets. There are no bowling analyses, but it would seem Clarke acted purely as a batsman. The Hon E.Lascelles had invited Mr Mynn and Mr Denison and as many All-England players as were available to spend the day after the Leeds match at Harewood Park – in fact only the umpire Caldecourt and apparently Sherman came; an informal match took place in Harewood Park. Cricket did not end with the Swaffham match; on 21 and 22 September, at Hyde Park in Sheffield, Clarke and George Butler played a single-wicket match for £25 against Thomas Hunt and Samuel Baldwinson. A day later the same pairs travelled to Moss Lane, Manchester for a return match. The Manchester players won both games. The second match was also for £25, proving an expensive end of season for Clarke and Butler.

It is worth noting that, with Clarke no longer at the Trent Bridge Inn, no important matches were staged on the adjoining ground during the season. A friendly opening match on 25 May – single-innings and one-day – resulted in the solitary comment, 'attendance very poor', though George Parr played and scored 97. The next reported match was on Whit Monday, 1 June. John Chapman with 31 was the highest scorer. Tentative arrangements for Nottingham to play Cambridge were made, but the game was cancelled as Cambridge withdrew. 27 July saw the annual Town v County contest; John Chapman appeared for the Town, the Inn having this curious situation of being half in and half out of the town.

A Gentlemen v Players game was arranged for Trent Bridge for 3 August, but it was rained off. It was re-arranged for a week later. John Chapman appeared for the Gentlemen, but was described as a professional. The Trent Bridge season closed with Physic v Law on 3 September – an innings of 41 by T.B.Redgate gave Law victory. The principal reported sporting activity on Trent Bridge ground during the winter months around this time was pigeon shooting.

George Parr, who was noted as being absent from the three initial England matches, of course merits more than a passing comment, since his place beside Clarke was to be so prominent in future seasons. He was born at Radcliffe on Trent in 1826, and the following description was written in 1853 by J.F.Sutton:

He is undoubtedly the first batsman in the country, and for brilliancy and precision of striking has never been surpassed. He occupies now the same commanding position that Fuller Pilch did, some ten or fifteen years since; with this difference, that Pilch, though a powerful and most dexterous batter, never possessed the grace and finish displayed by the subject of this notice. Parr excels greatly in leg hits. Were there no such thing as leg-hitting, we should see a full bat every time the ball came, with the batsman steady on his legs and only one thing to think of, and what a task a bowler would have! It is generally the upright straight players that weary a bowler – twenty-two inches of wood by four-and-a-quarter – every inch of them before the stumps, batting or blocking, it is that that is rather discouraging; but the moment a man makes ready for a leg-hit, the bat points to slip instead of to bails and only about five inches by four of wood covers the wicket; so leg-hitting, with ordinary players, is the bowler's chance; cutting, also, for a similar reason. But not so with George Parr; so unerring is his aim, he gives the bowler as little chance with the leg-hit as with any other, and punishes both ball, bowler and lyers-out, with an ease perfectly marvellous. Parr is one of the chief attractions of the All England Eleven; and no first-rate match can be considered complete without his services.

Earlier, in 1849, Fred Lillywhite describes Parr as the celebrated bat and the 'England Pet'.

Apart from Parr, a second player who missed out on the three 1846 matches, but whom Clarke had wanted in his team, was Nicholas Felix. He joined in 1847 and with Parr was then a regular. Like Alfred Mynn, Felix, being in theory an amateur, was paid 'expenses' by Clarke. Felix's financial affairs were not quite as awry as Mynn's, but not far off! Born in Camberwell in 1804, he took over as headmaster of Alfred House Academy when his father, the previous headmaster, died in 1824; the school moved from Camberwell to Blackheath in 1832, but his enthusiasm for cricket slowly overtook his enthusiasm for teaching and it seems that he abandoned the latter in 1847, when the programme of All-England matches expanded. In or about 1848 he was appointed President of the All-England Eleven, though Clarke remained in total control of the finances of the team. Felix (real name Wanostrocht) had made his debut for Gentlemen v Players in 1831 and continued to appear in those games until 1852. Living in Blackheath he played for Kent from 1834 to 1852. Caffyn describes his cricket:

He was a beautiful bat (left-hand), being especially noted for his brilliant cutting, more particularly in the direction of cover-point (with the right leg in his case advanced). Mr Felix was undoubtedly one of the very finest exponents of this stroke ever seen. I have seen no batsman from W.G.Grace downwards who could excel him in this particular. Being a left-handed bat, he had ample opportunities of indulging in this favourite hit of his, as most of the bowlers in those days did not change sides of the wicket when bowling to a left-handed man; and as they bowled round the wicket in most cases with a break from leg, a batsman like Felix had only to wait for a slightly over-tossed ball to punish it severely.

Felix had published in 1845 an excellent book, entitled *Felix on the Bat*, an instructional work, which contained many excellent illustrations – he was a noted artist and carried his sketch pad and paints on his tours with All-England. In the two seasons of 1851 and 1852, Felix, during his travels with Clarke's team, wrote reports on many of the matches. Some of these reports found their way into *Bell's Life*. Felix also kept notes on the team's off-the-field activities and in many cases produced water-colour sketches of the venues used by the team. It was his intention to publish this material as a book, but this did not occur. The diaries, notes and sketches came into the possession of MCC in 1944. Gerald Brodribb, whilst researching his biography of Felix, was able to study the material and determined that it should be published. Brodribb's edited version was published by Boundary Books in 2002. Sad to relate, Gerald Brodribb died in 1999 and therefore never saw the finished volume.

Chapter Eight

Incredible Success of the All-England Eleven

In that initial year of 1846, Clarke had arranged just three matches, detailed in the previous chapter. In 1847 the number rose to ten (MCC's fixture list amounted to 18); in 1848 to 16 (MCC 16); in 1849 to 21 (MCC 12); in 1850 to 24 (MCC 17); and in 1851 to 34 (MCC 16). The majority of MCC matches were played at Lord's and very few of the remainder were staged outside the traditional, southern home of cricket.

By 1851, therefore, Clarke was organizing twice as many matches as MCC and, of course, having no 'home' ground, these were spread across the whole of England from Newcastle to Teignbridge, plus matches in Glasgow and Edinburgh. The importance of the rapidly expanding railway system cannot be too strongly emphasized in looking at the spread of Clarke's fixture list, both in numbers and geographically – the map on page 70 has been included to demonstrate this point. In terms of popularity and the demand from clubs to stage All-England matches, the nearest, perhaps the only, comparison must surely be the Australian touring sides of the 1880s before the tourists' fixtures were governed by, effectively, the M.C.C. In both cases the owners or controllers of the individual venues saw that a large profit could be made. The nearest modern-day equivalent, on a much smaller scale, is the clamour by county grounds to climb on to the Test/International bandwagon.

Of course the railways were paramount, but Richard Daft in *Kings of Cricket* tells a rather sad railway tale, probably dating from near the end of Clarke's career:

> Once, too, a railway porter tried to get him [Clarke] to leave a non-smoking compartment in which he was enjoying a cigar, and which at first Clarke refused to quit. The porter, placing one hand on the window-sill, waved the other to call the attention of the station-master; and while so engaged, Clarke clapped the lighted end of his cigar on the back of his hand. The official sent up a howl, but Clarke coolly told him he was merely extinguishing his weed as he had been bidden and if any harm had come of it, it must be entirely owing to the owner of the hand and not to the owner of the cigar.

Humour was rather more robust in those less delicate times.

Clarke in 1847 retained his post as a 'ground bowler' at Lord's and as such was extensively used by MCC in their matches – he played in a dozen games between the last week of May and the second week of August when the MCC season virtually closed. Clarke, in his team's second summer, therefore arranged his fixtures from mid-August onwards. The first of the ten All-England Eleven matches commenced at the Wharf Street Ground

The famous Nicholas Felix drawing of 1847, showing the All-England Eleven of that year. From l to r: J.Guy, G.Parr, W.Martingell, A.Mynn, W.Denison, J.Dean sr, W.Clarke, N.Felix, O.C.Pell, W.Hillyer, F.W.Lillywhite, W.Dorrinton, F.Pilch, T.Sewell sr.
(Later the side wore shirts with red spots, hence the back cover of this book.)

in Leicester, the venue of the famous North v South match of 1836, on 12 August. England won by an innings and most significantly George Parr hit exactly 100 on this, his All-England debut. He, together with Nicholas Felix, both appeared for the first time after unavoidable absences in 1846.

Parr and Felix were the obvious additions to Clarke's team, but one curiosity of the 1847 All-England team was the inclusion of Oliver Claude Pell, who was the opposing captain to V.S.C.Smith in the 1847 University match at Lord's. Pell played in the first seven of the ten 1847 AEE matches and in two matches the following year, after which he gave up serious cricket to concentrate on the law, qualifying as a barrister. Pell was notable for his fielding and his powerful throwing arm. Born in Middlesex in 1825, he was in the Rugby eleven and then four years in the Cambridge side. Residing near Ely he played a few games for Cambridge Town Club. More famous for his expertise in rifle-shooting, he was, for three years, a member of the England team in this sport.

Joining the AEE for Pell's final match of 1847 and appearing in the other three games was Pell's colleague in the Cambridge side, T.M.Townley, who played under the alias of Mr England! He achieved little and soon disappeared from major cricket after the 1848 University game.

William Lillywhite, whose name had been advertised in several papers as a member of the All-England Eleven in 1846, finally made his debut in the sixth match of 1847, versus Sheffield at Hyde Park. The Sheffield paper describes the match in great detail, including, in the morning prior to play, some apt comments on the principal players:

> Soon after eleven, an unusual bustle near the entrance gate betokened something of importance, and in few seconds the well-remembered forms of the All England players were seen in the distance, carrying their implements of war, the almost colossal figures of Mr Mynn and Pilch towering above the rest. We immediately recognized the immortal Lillywhite from his portrait, which almost every cricketer has seen; and a certain working of the shoulders and a bustling hurried step bespoke the indefatigable Jemmy Dean. The veteran Clarke too was easily distinguished by his well-known plodding gait. The whole of the All England players appeared in remarkably good health and spirits.

Unfortunately for Clarke England were dismissed for 64, the wickets falling to Skelton and Barker who bowled unchanged. They owed even this modest total largely to Clarke, who went in at No.8 and was not out 11 when the last wicket, that of Lillywhite, fell. The Eighteen of Sheffield made 126, Lillywhite taking most of the early wickets and returning figures of six for 50; Martingell mopped up the tail with six for 14: Clarke only bowled five overs. Clarke chose to open the batting in the second innings. He performed the unusual feat of hitting a six, the report noting: 'Clarke afterwards made a tremendous leg hit from Mr Barker, for which he was marked six, the ball going over the outer wall on the low side of the ground. A well-merited round of applause followed the performance of this feat.' This emphasizes that to score a six without having to run, the ball had to be hit right out of the ground. Unless there was an agreement

*The All-England Eleven match venues 1846-1856, and the railways
in operation in 1850. Clarke made good use of new technology –
in his case, the railways – like any twenty-first century entrepreneur.*

on a particular ground regarding 'booth' balls, then all runs were actually run.

Clarke scored 22 in all, but the total was a poor 71 and Sheffield won the game by 17 wickets – one of the worst defeats the AEE ever suffered. Lillywhite was aged 55 at the time of this match and very near the end of his long career. He played five matches for the AEE in 1848 and one final game in 1849. He was to die in 1854, two years before Clarke. The Barker mentioned in the Sheffield team was not Tom Barker of Nottingham, but Thomas Rawson Barker, born in Bakewell in 1812 and a lead merchant in Sheffield; he was later Mayor of that town.

The other Sussex bowler to make a first appearance for the side was John Wisden, but he was not a regular member of the eleven until 1849, so will be discussed in that season. The overall results – won three, lost three and four drawn – were not too impressive, but in no way affected the public interest in the team. Clarke certainly broke new ground in taking the AEE to Newcastle and Stockton.

Pycroft in *The Cricket Field* recalls the following comments made by James Dark:

> Soon after that [*i.e.* the formation of the AEE] I heard of Clarke with the same eleven having made a match against some side at Newcastle, where as I told Clarke, there were no players at all fit to stand against him. 'Never you mind,' replied Clarke, 'I shall play sides, strong or weak, with numbers or with bowlers given, and shall play all over the country too – mark my words – and it will make good for cricket and for your trade too.' ... And sure enough the increase in my bat-and-ball trade bears witness to Clarke's long-sighted speculation.

Allied to the subsequent boom in sales of cricket equipment, due to Clarke's pioneering fixtures, came the demand for professional cricketers. Before the mid-1840s the number of salaried positions available to talented cricketers was very, very limited. The MCC at Lord's employed a handful, while what few organized counties there were to that date simply paid players per match, except that Fuller Pilch at Town Malling received an annual payment of £100. Eton College signed their first professional, Sam Redgate, in 1840, but it was not until the 1850s that public schools in general began to believe that a cricket professional was a vital piece of school equipment.

Similarly, well-to-do local cricket clubs started to sort out good quality professionals rather than just employ a local man to act as a general factotum to the club. Clarke's enterprise played a major part in this growth in cricket professionals: indeed one might with justification say that Clarke created the modern professional player/coach.

Returning to that notable Newcastle game, the local side included Barker and Skelton, the bowlers who had caused the AEE such trouble in Sheffield, and the game itself was an even draw. The match was organized by the Northumberland Club, a social club which organized cricket matches for its members and had a cricket ground on Bath Road. When the club decided to invite the All-England Eleven, there were invitations sent out to the great and good of the area inviting them to become patrons of the club, and the Duke of Northumberland was among those who responded positively to the call 'in handsome terms', according to the *Newcastle Journal.* The same paper gives this amusing description of Alfred Mynn:

> In Mr Mynn, the spectator beholds a tall, fine robust figure, somewhat corpulent and weighing at least eighteen stone, with feeding qualities, that, but for active exercise, would soon increase to thirty. He has a handsome, intelligent countenance, a noble bearing and commanding aspect. His pecuniary means are understood to be ample and like a true English gentleman, he is fond of the sport.

Another note on the match states that the billiard room of the Club was given up as a dressing apartment for the All-England party.

The Newcastle match was paired with a game at Stockton-on-Tees during the second half of the same week – Stockton was a much more notable cricketing venue. Perhaps Dark's comment was made in 1846, not 1847, because the *Manchester Courier* of 9 September 1846, reporting on the first day's play of the AEE v Manchester game, states: 'The All England gentlemen, we believe, would play on Monday and Tuesday at Leeds, whence they will proceed to Newcastle and Edinburgh, at both of which places they have engagements to fulfil.'

Most of the All-England team, though not Clarke, made the long journey from Stockton to Brighton for a four-day game, England v Sussex. It proved to be the final major contest on the ground set out by the Prince of Wales and latterly run by Thomas Box. Part of the ground was sold for building during the winter of 1847/48. Nottinghamshire, led by Clarke, had played their first inter-county match there in 1835. There was a break of a week and the season closed with the AEE match v Stourbridge on 4, 5 and 6 October.

William Clarke, as far as can be gauged, steered clear of his native county in 1847. John Chapman continued to run the Trent Bridge ground and was no doubt cheered when on 9 April 1847, the newly formed Nottingham Commercial Club decided to base their activities there. Pedestrian races were staged on the ground on 22 May, but the report notes 'poor attendance'. A Nottingham XI played Burton upon Trent at Trent Bridge on 29 May – the Nottingham side including Samuel and William Chapman.

There are no reports or scores of either Town v County or Gentlemen v Players games at Trent Bridge in 1847. One assumes these two long-standing annual contests no longer commanded the interest of the paying spectators. The major match on the ground was Thomas Barker's Benefit on 9, 10 and 11 August 1847 when Nottinghamshire opposed England. Haygarth in his notes is very scathing of the visiting side: ' ... the England Eleven was a *very* inferior one ... in fact it had no right to assume that name ... the match was evidently got up by some party at Nottingham who either could not collect the talent of the country, or else wished to secure an easy victory for his own party.'

Clarke was conspicuous by his absence; he and other notables were in fact appearing on the same days in the Sussex v MCC match at Brighton, Clarke being part of the MCC team. John Chapman scored 28 for Nottinghamshire who won by ten wickets.

With the Trent Bridge Ground at a low ebb and the town of Nottingham beginning its expansion outside the traditional 'town walls', especially in the fields to the south and thus towards the River Trent, it is surprising that at some point between 1850 and 1890 the builders didn't take over the Trent Bridge Ground itself. The first reason was that the freehold owners of almost all of West Bridgford, the Musters family based at Colwick Hall, which stood on the north bank facing Gamston across the river, but also owning Bridgford Hall (in West Bridgford), would not release any land for development in the village. By the time that they had decided to do so – in the late 1880s and 1890s – the County Cricket Club was at its most prosperous. In 1885 the Club had demolished and rebuilt the Trent Bridge Inn; the following year the Club took the lease of an extra piece of land on the south side of the ground opposite the pub and built what at the time was the most palatial cricket pavilion in England. Within a few years the expanded ground was surrounded by houses, but the importance of the cricket ground had now been firmly established – in addition to cricket, Notts County Football Club, a founding member of the Football League, used the Fox Road side of the ground for its matches until 1910.

Clarke continued at Lord's in 1848, even though he arranged an additional six AEE matches. He appeared in a thirteen-a-side practice match on the ground on 22 May and then an unusual fixture among MCC members and professionals, Under-hand v Round-arm, on 5 June. His first serious game was for North v MCC at Lord's on 12 and 13 June, when he took 13 wickets for the North. He played for MCC v Surrey Club at The Oval two days later. In 1846 and 1847 he had deliberately held back his AEE matches until after the Canterbury Festival; however, this summer he squeezed two AEE fixtures in a gap in MCC's match programme, taking the England side to Birmingham and Worcestershire during the week commencing 19 June. It was fresh territory for the travelling professionals.

Making his debut for Clarke's team in these early games was Tom Box. He had been the Sussex wicketkeeper since 1826 and was aged 40 when making his first appearance for the AEE. Despite his rather advanced age, Box was to be a regular in the team until 1855. Caffyn comments: 'Like most wicketkeepers of that time he set himself to look after the off-balls and allowed the leg ones, to a great extent, to look after themselves.' In 1847 he had given up the old 'Prince of Wales' ground in Brighton, part of which was sold for housing. He then ran the Egremont Hotel in the town. Later on he worked on Prince's Ground in Chelsea, dying whilst working the scoreboard on the ground during the Middlesex v Nottinghamshire match of 1876. The match was abandoned as a sign of respect for the old cricketer. Clarke obviously valued Box's experience and Box was appointed, more or less on his match debut, as a member of the AEE committee.

Later in the season Clarke arranged another two AEE matches in the MCC

Clarke, now fifty and looking well fed, by Felix in 1848.

fixtures gap between the Gentlemen v Players match at Lord's and Kent playing England at Canterbury. (The Public Schools matches were staged at Lord's during this time.) AEE opposed West Kent at Gravesend and Surrey at The Oval. It was perhaps an over-optimistic indulgence to allow Surrey in the latter contest, to field 14 men against the England Eleven, especially as Surrey fielded several of Clarke's players – Martingell, Sewell, Felix and Hinkly. On the other hand the new Surrey County Cricket Club had only begun to play matches in 1846 and was to an extent an unknown quantity. The county duly won by eight wickets.

Immediately before the Surrey game, Clarke's team opposed Fifteen of West Kent, with two given men, at Gravesend. Haygarth states the match was on the Bat and Ball Ground, but Howard Milton in his history of Kent grounds notes that the Bat and Ball ground was not opened until the following year. To add to the confusion, the match is not connected to the long-established West Kent Cricket Club, which was based at Chislehurst.

Clarke maintained his commitment to MCC by playing as part of the England side, organized by MCC, against Kent during the Canterbury festival. Directly after that event there was a clash of fixtures. Nottingham played Sheffield at Trent Bridge on the same dates as the All-England Eleven played Twenty-Two of Coventry. Guy and George Parr turned out for Nottingham, whereas Clarke stayed with the All-England Eleven. Nottingham were beaten; All-England won by two wickets, Clarke taking ten wickets in the first innings and a further six in the second. A little-known cricketer called Belsom played for England, batting at No.11 and failing to score in each innings. It would appear that he was a last-minute replacement, perhaps for Parr. However Clarke was seemingly not upset by Parr's absence, for he returned to the England side in the game the following Monday at Derby and made the highest score, 25. The press commented that Parr batted six hours, which even in those slow-scoring times might have created a record, but on checking the detail, the time included long stoppages for rain. The match was a benefit for Sam Dakin, who was the professional for the local club and had played once for Nottinghamshire in 1845. A number of the All-England matches were arranged as benefits, though I have been unable to discover exactly how the money was divided between Clarke and the beneficiary. It would seem most unlikely that Clarke would provide his services and those of his players free of charge! The final AEE game of the season was another such benefit, for Daniel Day, on the ground he ran at Itchen, Southampton, when England opposed fourteen of Hampshire. In the previous week the

BY AUTHORITY.—J. & F. LILLYWHITE'S REGISTER
OF
THE ALL ENGLAND CRICKET MATCHES FOR 1848.
AT HYDE PARK, SHEFFIELD.   August 28th 29th & 30th.
Sixteen of Sheffield v. Eleven of All England.   3rd day   o'clock.

Sheffield	1st innings		2nd do.
M. J. Ellison, esq	b Clarke	1 .. c Box, b Martingell	11
Hunt	c Dean, b Hinkly	6 .. b Hinkly	11
Chatterton	b do	21 .. b Martingell	5
R. Wake, esq	b do	0 .. c Mynn, b Martingell	7
Coates	c W. Pilch, b Mynn	11 .. c Box, b Dean	5
Sampson	b Mynn	35 .. b Hinkly	7
T. E. Barker, esq	b Mynn	7 .. c Hoare, b Martingell	5
Wright	b Mynn	12 .. run out	5
R. F. Skelton, esq	b Mynn	3 .. b Martingell	1
Hurt	b Dean	0 .. c King, b Martingell	3
B. Huntsman, esq	b Dean	0 .. c Felix, b Martingell	3
T. Hall	c King, b Clarke	5 .. b Hinkly	2
Thompson	c Dean, b do	10 .. c King, b Martingell	0
J. Vincent	b Mynn	0 .. run out	1
Biggins	not out	3 .. b Hinkly	0
Mr Worrall	l b w, b Mynn	0 .. not out	1
	b 2, w 2, nb	4	b l, w 4, nb	5
	Total	**118**	**Total**	**77**

England	1st innings		2nd do.
W. Pilch	c Wright, b Skelton	4 .. b Barker	13
Clarke	b do	1 .. b Wright	5
Martingell	l b w, b do	2 .. b Skelton	20
R. T. King, esq	b Barker	0 .. c Huntsman, b Wright	10
Parr	c Wake, b Skelton	20 .. b Skelton	0
Box	c Coates, b do	3 .. b Skelton	7
N. Felix, esq	b Barker	5 .. c do b Wright	8
A. Mynn, esq	not out	11 .. b Skelton	1
C. H. Hoare, esq	b Skelton	1 .. run out	3
Dean	b Wright	0 .. not out	2
Hinkly	b Wright	8 .. run out	13
	b 2, w 6, nb		b 4, w 9, nb	
	Total	**58**	**Total**	**82**

The Lillywhite scorecard of the Sheffield XVI match against the All-England XI played at Hyde Park, Sheffield in late August 1848. Clarke seems to have opened the AEE batting and bowling but his side lost by 55 runs.

AEE had played at Leamington. George Parr played in this match –he only missed one AEE game all season. In the penultimate game, John Wisden played as a given man against the AEE, then appeared for Clarke's side in the game at Itchen. Wisden and Parr clearly became friends because in the winter of 1848/49 they jointly took over the ground at Leamington and Wisden moved house from Brighton to the Spa town.

A comment was made above regarding the clash of dates of the AEE fixtures and Nottingham. With John Chapman in charge of Trent Bridge, it is obvious that Clarke was not welcome. Chapman had made a great effort in 1848 to organize some major matches on the ground and at least obtained home and away fixtures with Sussex and Sheffield. However, there are no cricket references in the *Nottingham Review* between 1 March and 17 June to any fixtures arranged at Trent Bridge. The first reported game was on 17 and 18 July and is described as Nottinghamshire v Leicestershire, though in fact it was the Notts Amateur Club, reinforced by George Parr – Leicester were beaten by an innings and 12 runs. The return game in Leicester was played under the odd title of Trent Bridge (Nottingham) Club v Leicestershire. A note on the Nottingham v Sheffield match states that Mr Chapman lost £40 owing to a payment to the Sheffield players and the lack of support. The return game against Sussex was played as late as 18, 19 and 20 September and was left unfinished because half the Sussex team had to travel to Brighton to start a match on 21 September – Brighton v Mitcham. Nottinghamshire were in dire straits when the match ended, being nearly 300 runs in arrears and Sussex still having one wicket to fall in their second innings. No fewer than eight bowlers were tried in Sussex's second innings. The fixture clashed with another AEE match. It is almost superfluous to state Clarke did not play in any of the four major Notts games organized by John Chapman.

The 1849 season saw Clarke increase his appearances on the cricket field. He took part in 31 matches published in *Scores and Biographies* and Lillywhite's averages for 1849 credit him with 267 wickets; only Hillyer, who played in an additional eight matches, had more wickets that season with 358. John Wisden exactly equalled Clarke's wicket tally, though he appeared in only 26 matches. No doubt due to Wisden's partnership with Parr, the Sussex bowler became a regular member of the AEE for 1849, but he was an independent-minded person and his relationship with Clarke was neither long nor happy – later he was to join forces with Lillywhite, though again the working relationship did not survive the test of time. Caffyn describes Wisden as a 'particularly keen man of business'. As a fast bowler, he proved a great asset to the All-England team and bowling in harness with Clarke dismissed the twenty-twos with great ease. V.E.Walker, the Middlesex cricketer, described Wisden as 'a funny little mite of a fellow'; his height is given as 5ft 4in, very small for a round-arm bowler of his pace.

In 1848 the first AEE game hadn't taken place until June, but in 1849, Clarke's side dominated the principal fixtures for May. Starting at Durham on 3 May, the touring side moved on to Edinburgh, then Bedale, then Rugby and finally Cambridge, all in that month. The Scotland match was played on the Grange Ground and W.Moncrieff, in *Reminiscences of the Grange Cricket Club, Edinburgh, 1832-62,* comments:

> In 1849 the famous Eleven of England made their first appearance in Scotland on the Grange Ground, against Twenty-two of Scotland, including some professionals. They had an easy victory, but the match created quite a sensation; people flocked from all parts of Scotland to witness it, and its effects were to bring new life into Cricket in Scotland. Clubs were formed in all directions; professionals were engaged from England; and in a few years play all round was wonderfully improved.

With Wisden playing for the AEE, the first four games ended in victory, before a draw against Cambridge Town Club at Fenner's – in fact a benefit for Fenner. Neither Clarke nor Wisden turned out, possibly in the case of Clarke because he was required as a practice bowler at Lord's. Four places in the AEE side at Cambridge were filled by local amateurs. MCC had arranged their first match of the Lord's season to be Fast Bowlers v Slow Bowlers commencing 28 May. Due to rain the game did not begin until the following day – Wisden, opening the batting for Fast, was caught and bowled by Clarke without scoring. Wisden's bowling though won the match for the Fast men. He took 12 wickets; Clarke took seven for the Slows. The next game at Lord's was Married v Single, with Clarke part of the Married, and Wisden, the Single. Clarke hit the highest score in the game, scoring 71 before being run out (he was aged 50), but Wisden again triumphed with 12 dismissals and Single won by three wickets.

Cricket.

THE MATCH

BETWEEN THE

ELEVEN of ENGLAND

AND EIGHTEEN OF THE

COUNTY of DORSET,

Will be played at the Ground of the

PYMORE CRICKET CLUB,

NEAR BRIDPORT,

On MONDAY, 19th AUGUST next, & following days

The Wickets will be pitched at 11, A.M.

The usual Ordinary Dinner will take place at 3 o'clock. Tickets 2s. 6d. each.

ENGLAND.	DORSET.	
A. MYNN, Esq.	H. VERNON, Esq.	H. TEMPLER, Esq.
N. FELIX, Esq.	W. HOUNSELL, Esq.	R. TEMPLER, Esq.
ADAMS	J. STUCKEY, Esq.	T. JOHNS, Esq.
CLARKE	B. GUNDRY, Esq.	H. TURNER, Esq.
CHATTERTON	F. COMPTON, Esq.	A. MANSELL, Esq.
GUY	F. COMPTON, Esq.	BELL
HILLYER	W. HOOPER, Esq.	BROWN
HUNT	T. P. WICKHAM, Esq.	MARTIN
MARTINGELL	CAPT. MAYO	DAY.
PARR		
F. PILCH.		
Umpire, BAYLEY.	*Umpire,* BOODLE.	

Charge for Admission to Non-Contributors, 6d. each. Carriages, 1s. It is a particular request that Visitors keep outside of the Bounds of the Flag and abstain from Remaining or Walking in a line with the Wickets.

Lillywhite's Printing Press will be on the Ground, where the Score can be obtained at any minute of the Game.

TUCKER, BROTHER, BRIDPORT.

The circus comes to town. Handbill for All-England match against a Dorset XVIII played just outside Bridport in August 1850. AEE had played a XXII at Hereford a couple of days before, and moved on to Southampton straight after this game.

There is a most interesting diagram in Pycroft's *The Cricket Field* comparing Clarke's bowling with Wisden's. Pycroft then starts his following chapter, entitled 'Bowling – An Hour with "Old Clarke"', spelling out Clarke's skills as bowler and tactician, with the following comments:

> In cricket wisdom Clarke is truly 'Old': what he has learnt from anybody, he learnt from Lambert. But he is a man who thinks for himself, and knows men and manners. 'I beg your pardon, sir,' he one day said to a gentleman taking guard, 'but ain't you Harrow?' 'Then we shan't want a man down there.' He said, addressing a fieldman; 'stand for the "Harrow drive", between point and middle wicket.'

> The time to see Clarke is the morning of a match. While others are practising, he walks round with his hands under the flaps of his coat, reconnoitering his adversaries' wicket. 'Before you bowl to a man, it is worth something to know what is running in his head. That gentleman', he will say, 'is too fast on his feet, so, as good as ready money to me: if he doesn't hit he can't score; if he does I shall have him.'

> Going a little further, he sees a man lobbing to another, who is practising stepping in. 'There, sir, is "practising to play Clarke", that

is very plain; and a nice mess, you will see, he will make of it. Ah! My friend, if you do go in at all, you must go in further than that, or my twist will beat you; and going in to swipe around, eh! Learn to run me down with a straight bat, and I will say something to you. But that wouldn't score quite fast enough for your notions. Going in to hit round is a tempting of Providence.'

'There, that man is pure stupid; alter the pace and height with a dropping ball, and I shall have no trouble with him. They think, sir, it is nothing but "Clarke's vexatious pace": they know nothing about the curves. With fast bowling, you cannot have half my variety; and when you have found out the weak point, where's the fast bowler that can give the exact ball to hit it? There is often no more head-work in fast bowling than there is in the catapult; without head-work I should be hit out of the field.'

'A man is never more taken aback than when he prepares for one ball, and I bowl him the contrary one: there was Mr Nameless, the first time he came to Nottingham, full of fancies about playing me. The first ball he walked some yards out to meet me, and I pitched over his head, so near his wicket, that, thought I, that bird won't fight again. Next ball he was a little cunning, and made a feint of coming out, meaning, as I guessed, to stand back for a long hop; so I pitched right up to him; and he was so bent upon cutting me away, that he hit his own wicket down!'

'See, there,' continues Clarke, 'that gentleman's *is* a dodge certainly, but not a new one either. He does step in it is true; but while hitting at the ball, he is so anxious about getting back again, that his position has all the danger of stepping in, and none of its advantage.'

'Then there is Mr -------,' naming a *Great* man struggling with adversity. 'He gives a jump up off his feet, and thinks he is stepping in, but comes flump down just where he was before.' ... 'Pilch plays me better than anyone. But he knows better than to step in to every ball, or to stand fast every ball. He plays steadily, and discriminates, waiting till I give him a chance, and then makes the most of it.'

Clarke, in this fourth year of the All-England Eleven, was most careful to arrange his fixtures so that they did not clash with MCC-organized matches and the sequence of games over the next few weeks clearly demonstrates this:

18 and 19 June	England v Surrey	Lord's
21 and 22 June	AEE v Kent	Gravesend
25 and 26 June	MCC v Sussex	Lord's
28, 29 and 30 June	AEE v XIV of Hampshire	Southampton
9 and 10 July	England v Kent	Lord's
16 and 17 July	North v South	Lord's
19, 20 and 21 July	AEE v XXII of Hull	Hull
23 and 24 July	Players v Gentlemen	Lord's
26, 27 and 28 July	AEE v XXII of Newark	Newark

30, 31 July, 1 August	AEE v XX of Leicester	Leicester
2, 3 and 4 August	AEE v XVIII of Bury & Suffolk	Bury St Edmunds
6 and 7 August	Surrey v England (chosen by MCC)	Kennington Oval
9, 10 and 11 August	AEE v XVIII of Dorset	Weymouth
13 and 14 August	Sussex v MCC	Hove
20, 21 and 22 August	Kent v England (chosen by MCC)	Canterbury

James Dark, or more probably Roger Kynaston, who was both Hon Secretary and Treasurer of MCC, and Clarke were fully co-operating with each other. A year or two later however, Kynaston drew up some more draconian rules to govern professionals employed by MCC, and Clarke, so Ashley-Cooper states in *Lord's and the M.C.C.*, was not happy; he and Dorrinton resigned their posts.

In 1848, Clarke had included an amateur cricketer, R.T.King, in most of his AEE matches. In 1849, for the first half of his programme he selected Henry Lindow (1824-1887), educated at Rugby and Oxford. Haygarth thought Lindow a poor player, but in 1848, Lindow had played against the AEE for Worcestershire and hit the highest score for his side in Worcestershire's second innings; a few days later he made 23 out of Worcestershire's total of 49, facing the professional bowlers Nixon and Roby – George Parr played

CLOSE OF THE FIRST TWO INNINGS
Second Day, Tuesday, Aug. 14, 1849.

Marylebone and Sussex.

First Inn. MARYLEBONE.		2nd Inn.	
W. Nicholson, Esq. b by Wisden	1		· · ·
Clark, b by Wisden	9		· · ·
Chester, b by Wisden	0		· · ·
Hillyer, c Box b by Wisden	15		· · ·
Royston, L before wicket b Dean	11		· · ·
Diver, b by Dean	2		· · ·
R. Kynaston, Esq. c Dean b Wisden	3		· · ·
H. B. Mayne Esq. b by Dean	0		· · ·
M. Earl Esq. b. by Dean	1		· · ·
W. A. Ford Esq. b by Dean	0		· · ·
Lillywhite, not out	0		· · ·
Byes 4 No Balls	4	Byes No Balls	·
Leg Byes . Wide ditto	·	Leg Bys . Wd do	·
	46		·

First Inn. SUSSEX.		2nd Inn.	
G. W. King, Esq. b by Hillyer	0		· · ·
H. M. Curteis, Esq. b by Clark	1		· · ·
E. Napper, Esq. b by Hillyer	6		· · ·
W. Napper. Esq. b by Hillyer	17		· · ·
Bushby, b by Hillyer	3		· · ·
Picknell, st Nicholson b Hillyer	59		· · ·
Box, s by Nicholson b Clark	39		· · ·
Wisden, b by Lillywhite	13		· · ·
Dean, b by Lillywhite	0		· · ·
Hammond, b by Hillyer	1		· · ·
Medson, not out	0		· · ·
Byes 3 No Balls 1	4	Byes . No Balls	·
Leg Byes . Wide ditto	·	Leg Bys . Wd do	·
	143		·

Marquees and Booths, for Fetes, &c. on hire, apply at G. Mant's, Birdham, Sussex.
Published at the close of every Wicket, at the end of each day's play, and at the close of the game, by G. Mant, at his Fruit & Confectionery Stall. Printed on the Ground by Phillips & Co. Poplar-place, Brighton.

Second-day scorecard published by Phillips and Co of the match Sussex v MCC,
played on the seafront Brunswick Ground at Hove in August 1849.
John Wisden took thirteen wickets in all and gave Sussex a win by ten wickets.

for the opposition in the latter match. Perhaps Haygarth's assessment of Lindow was a trifle unfair. Lindow left the AEE team after the eighth match, being replaced by William Lautour (1812-1899). Lautour had arranged for the AEE to play a match on his own ground in Weymouth against Dorset. Left-handed both as a batsman and bowler, he played in several matches for MCC between 1845 and 1847.

Why did Clarke include these amateurs? One reason could have been simply to save money, but more likely the presence of wealthy amateurs improved the gravitas of the team. A third amateur, Alexander Marshall (1820-1871), one of three brothers closely connected with Surrey County Cricket Club, played once for the AEE in 1849, twice in 1850 and eight times in 1851, then occasionally in 1852 and 1853. He played as a batsman for Surrey in 14 matches between 1849 and 1857. It was not a total coincidence that Clarke captained the Nottinghamshire side that played Surrey on Marshall's private ground, Broadwater Park, near Godalming, in 1854. It was the only first-class county match ever staged at that venue. We can assume that these amateurs themselves gained prestige from playing alongside the leading practitioners of their time.

Two professionals playing regularly for the first time in AEE ranks in 1849 were John Wisden and George Chatterton. Both had played the odd game earlier. Wisden took the place of Dean, whilst Chatterton replaced Dorrinton. Chatterton was, like Dorrinton, a good batsman and a wicketkeeper; he stood behind the stumps for Yorkshire, but had little opportunity in that position for the AEE, due to the presence of Box – he played frequently for Clarke's side only in 1849 and 1850 since in 1851 he joined the groundstaff at Lord's and remained there for 14 seasons.

After the first three seasons of trial and error, when he allowed the opposition varying numbers of players with the results quite often going against the All-England Eleven, Clarke in 1849 appeared to gauge the opposition's strength with more accuracy. Of the 21 matches he arranged, the AEE won 14, five were rain-affected draws and just two ended in defeat. One of these was against Derbyshire when R.C.Tinley, later to be a regular in the AEE ranks, caused problems as a bowler; the other was at Newark, when Tinley again proved the vehicle for England's downfall, taking nine AEE wickets in the first innings, with his brothers, Vincent and Frank, being the two highest scoring Newark batsmen!

Though Clarke was busier than ever, things were very quiet on the Trent Bridge Ground. John Chapman scored 58 for Notts Amateurs v Leicester on Barker's Ground at Leicester, but the only major game played at Trent Bridge in the season seems to have been Gentlemen of Nottinghamshire and Leicestershire v I Zingari on 9 and 10 August. I Zingari had been founded in 1845 and in 1849 greatly expanded their fixture list, which included many new matches in the Midlands. The club played on Parr and Wisden's ground at Leamington two or three days prior to the Trent Bridge match. It is believed that the home side was unique – never again did the Gentlemen of Nottinghamshire and Leicestershire raise a joint eleven. John Chapman did not play in the combined team.

During the 1849 season, the All-England Eleven started to play eleven-a-side fixtures. In the first of these, a drawn match at Fenner's against a Cambridge team, Clarke's side included Tom Box, William Martingell and George Parr.

Lillywhite's Guide to Cricketers 1851, which annual covers the summer of 1850, provides this pen portrait of William Clarke:

> Clarke, William, the celebrated slow bowler, was born at Nottingham in 1798. He is the able Secretary of the All England Eleven, and arranges all their matches. Clarke has been instrumental in promoting the game of cricket to its present height in the North of England.

Expanding the All-England Eleven matches by a further three fixtures for 1850, Clarke made a very early start to the season with a game in Carlisle beginning on 1 April. He also allowed the home sides in most matches to employ generally two or three 'given' men. In the case of XXII of Carlisle, the side was aided by Charles Lawrence, G.H.Wright and George Anderson. They were the first three bowlers used by Carlisle and took seven of the nine AEE wickets that fell to bowlers; in addition Wright and Lawrence were two of only four batsmen to achieve a double-figure score. Despite this help, Carlisle still lost by an innings. Clarke's side then moved north to Edinburgh to oppose XXII of Scotland, building on the tremendous success the 1849 visit had generated.

The All-England Eleven of 1850 showed little change from the regulars of 1847 – Clarke, Pilch, Mynn, Guy, Martingell, Hillyer, Felix and Parr, plus Box, the regular keeper from 1848. Wisden and Chatterton who had made frequent appearances in 1849 retained their places. The only new regular player in 1850 was Thomas Adams, who usually played in place of Pilch, perhaps because the latter, due to his Kent contract, was available for only 11 games. Fred Lillywhite's contemporary note on Adams reads: 'Thomas Adams was born at Gravesend in 1815; stands 5ft 10in. He is a very severe hitter and a very good bowler, and is in the habit of delivering the ball over the wicket. This season he has taken a house and ground at Ipswich.' He was actually born in 1813 – another example of a professional cricketer trimming a year or two off his age – the note regarding his bowling over the wicket is made because most round-arm bowlers delivered round the wicket during these years.

Although William Caffyn played in only four AEE matches 1850, becoming a regular in 1851, he requires some note, if simply because his reminiscences, *71 Not Out*, provide such a wealth of information on the All-England players. The book was published in 1899, many years after Clarke had died. Caffyn was born in Reigate in 1828 and played for Surrey from 1849 to 1873, but when he toured Australia with Parr's 1863/64 side, Caffyn decided to stay in Australia and his coaching had much to do with the improvement of Australian players and specifically those in New South Wales. He returned to England in 1871. Fred Lillywhite notes that Caffyn (in 1850) had a brilliant style of batting and was a very good bowler.

Caffyn's autobiography begins his piece on All-England and Clarke with:

> After this match [North v South on 15 July 1850, when John Wisden took all ten wickets], I was engaged by William Clarke (always known as 'Old Clarke') to play for his All-England Eleven at Cranbrook. A great and noble figure in the annals of our national games is this Old Clarke! A name to be honoured by all cricketers for all time. What an extraordinary and interesting career was his! ... Whatever may have been the slight failings as a man of this truly great cricketer (and I am bound to confess that he and myself did not get on too smoothly together), on looking back across a space of nearly half a century one is lost in admiration of this glorious veteran, who did perhaps more than any one else ever has done to popularize our great national game throughout the length and breadth of this country.

Caffyn continues by describing Clarke's bowling style and then goes on to comment on the rest of the matches in which he played during that summer of 1850, ending with the note:

> Playing so many matches and travelling so much was a great strain on one's constitution. We often had to travel all night and begin play at eleven o'clock on the morning we arrived at our place of destination, and I have often been so tired that I have almost fallen asleep while in the field. Clarke used to give us £4 a match at this time for the All-England matches.

The comprehensive volume, *The English Game of Cricket* by Charles Box, published in 1877, has some peculiar suggestions, made at great length, about cricket's early history, before Chapter 4 deals with the second quarter of the nineteenth century. Box comments:

> The movements of the All-England Eleven had a wonderful effect upon the cricket spirit of the age, for it not only introduced the game to places and peoples hitherto but very imperfectly acquainted with it, but served also to widen the sphere of its popularity to an extent not calculated upon. Wherever the foot of these chieftains trod they left the mark of cricket behind, and, without exception, the imprint remains to this day. ... Such was the success of Clarke, the chief manager of these matches, that other bands, imitating his example, convinced the world that professional cricket was not a bad vocation, although a danger of relying too much upon sunshine and smiles had

to be apprehended, and against which aspirants for fame, especially of this kind, were hardly equal. The advice of good men – such, for instance, as that of Mr Bass – was often found to be as the evening cloud and morning dew, and the prospects of many a young player of promise were prematurely blighted.

Box does not specifically mention that the spread of the railways had materially assisted in Clarke's ability to take his team to all corners of mainland Britain; however in 1877 readers would have been aware that railways had replaced stage coaches within living memory.

Clarke was still, in 1850, rather surprisingly a ground bowler at Lord's and played his first match for the Club on 3 and 4 June, appearing for MCC Professionals v XV of Middlesex. He played for England (selected by MCC) v Kent at Lord's on 8, 9 and 10 July, then in the famous North v South match at Lord's, when John Wisden took all ten wickets. Wisden, living at Leamington, played for the North, and the South were routed – all out for 36 and 76. In the first innings, Clarke and Wisden bowled unchanged, Clarke taking six wickets and Wisden three. Caffyn actually made the highest score in both of the South's innings, hence perhaps Clarke's reason for signing him up.

Clarke played at Lord's for Players v Gentlemen and in the unusually titled Young v Old match – Under-36 v Over-36. The Young won by 11 runs, but Haygarth commented that the Old might have succeeded if Mr Rogers had turned up to bat for them on the third day; seemingly he didn't realize that two-day matches at Lord's, if unfinished, were continued on a third day!

Clarke played in all 24 AEE matches in 1850; Parr missed one, but had a tremendous close to the season, hitting 118 v Amateurs of Sussex at Hove and in the next match 90 v Louth. The final AEE fixture went into the beginning of October, against XXII of Birmingham at Edgbaston.

The report of the match at Sheffield on 10 and 11 June 1850 comments on a quite astonishing innings by Bernard Wake, a local solicitor, that it deserves recognition. *The Sheffield and Rotherham Independent* reported:
> Mr Wake's appearance with bat in hand disturbed the compact arrangement of the fielders and signal was given for 'a spread'. Those who anticipated 'something smart' from him were not disappointed. After quickly making a single, he drove Wisden with tremendous force to the leg, where Parr, with his usual alacrity, gathered the ball and 'shied' it at the wicket, missing which, it was not stopped until another run was obtained from the overthrow. The ball was then overthrown a second and third time, Mr Wake having, in the meantime, amid the cheers and laughter of the assembled throng obtained five runs from this one stroke. The batting on the part of Mr Wake and Berry was of the most spirited character and adding most effectively to the score. A splendid hit from which Mr Wake ran five, disturbed the equanimity of 'The Old General' and a change of tactics was the result. Hillyer was succeeded in bowling by Clarke, who having 'planted' the field, commenced his first over to Mr Wake who drove him to the leg for two and the ball being overthrown in 'shying' at the wicket, three more

*A match between Sussex and the All-England Eleven being played at the
Royal Brunswick Ground on Hove seafront in 'about 1850', with the
St Andrew's Old Church in the background. In this fixture in 1849,
Clarke bowled through both Sussex innings and took twelve wickets;
the AEE won by an innings and 45 runs.*

*The match between an Ilkeston and District XXII and the All-England Eleven
under way in August 1851 at the Rutland Ground, Ilkeston.
Clarke bowled through both Ilkeston innings, securing eighteen victims,
and his side won by six wickets.*

runs obtained. Mr Wake immediately afterwards fell victim to one of Clarke's 'peculiars', which he played into the hands of Mynn. Mr Wake left the field loudly cheered after having in a very brief space of time obtained 19. His score consisted of three fives, a two and a couple of singles. ... Clarke's slow bowling did great execution, no less than nine of the thirteen wickets being taken from it. The fielding of the eleven in the early part of the innings, was not their usual effective character.

Clarke returned figures of nine for 34 off 20 overs in Yorkshire's first innings, the third time he had captured nine wickets in an innings in ACS-ranked first-class games. Caffyn commented on the team sometimes being half asleep after travelling overnight, but in this case, there was no match immediately prior to this one!

Between this appearance at Sheffield, when AEE lost, and their second appearance in September, the following letter was published in the *Nottingham Review:*

> Mr Editor,
>
> Having received a challenge from Mr Thomas Willey of Sheffield to play Twelve of Yorkshire against Eleven of England (bar myself) I accept the challenge and will play them on neutral ground halfway between London and Sheffield at Leamington, or the same eleven will play the same fourteen for the sum named – £100-a-side.
>
> Yours etc.
>
> W.Clark, Sec of All England Committee

Nothing seems to have come of this and when XV of Sheffield played the All-England Eleven at Hyde Park on 2, 3 and 4 September 1850, the AEE won by two wickets, despite the fact that Wisden was unable to bowl due to a sprained back.

Tom Sherman, the Surrey fast round-arm bowler, played a couple of matches for the AEE in 1850 and it is assumed that one of these provoked the following yarn of his regarding Clarke's payment to players at the close of each match:

> The cricketers went up to him one after the other for their money, and as I was the last in the row, I was able to take in all that transpired. Clarke had a heap of gold and silver in front of him, and during the paying-out process you would hear something like this: 'Four pounds for you, fifty shillings for you, three pounds for you,' the amounts varying according to the player's fame and what he had done in the match. When I approached him he looked up, saying: 'Fifty shillings for you,' and then, shoveling the balance into his trousers pockets, and giving a most satisfied smile, added, 'and thirty-seven pounds for me!'

Elsewhere Sherman tells how he was engaged as a professional for the local twenty-two and Clarke prevented him from bowling – Clarke, in other words dictating to the local clubs which professionals they could, or could not, include in their team when meeting the All-England Eleven.

There were no *bona fide* Notts County matches in 1850, though the Gentlemen of Nottinghamshire, based at Southwell, remained active. Both Nottingham Commercial and Notts Amateur Cricket Clubs played home matches at Trent Bridge during the season and these games are the only ones reported as taking place on that ground. John Chapman's name does not feature in a single Nottingham-based match – he may have moved to Gainsborough in 1850 – though his brother William Chapman appears once.

On 11 April 1851 the *Nottingham Review* reported: 'The following two matches have been made between Mr Houghton, proprietor of Kennington Oval and Mr Clark, the celebrated slow bowler: July 3, North v South; July 17, Surrey v Nottinghamshire.' From this notice it seemed that Clarke would be playing for Nottinghamshire during the coming season – his first appearance for the county since 1845, a gap of five years. However his fixtures for the All-England Eleven were to prove punishing, to say the least. He had arranged no fewer than 34 matches, the first on 5 May, the final one ending on 15 October, but still leaving spaces for the principal eleven-a-side matches arranged by MCC. The programme commenced with 13 fixtures end to end – in other words two three-day matches each week. When MCC matches were added, the major cricketers such as Clarke, Caffyn, Wisden and Parr, were scheduled to play in 43 or 44 matches, the only break being three days off in early August. William Caffyn comments in his reminiscences: 'I must acknowledge that I was heartily glad when the season of 1851 came to a close; indeed we all were, and looked forward with pleasure to a well-earned winter's rest.'

The first break for Clarke occurred much earlier, on 26, 27 and 28 May, when the All-England Eleven opposed XXII of Gainsborough. Opening the batting for Gainsborough was none other than his stepson, John Chapman. The 1851 census for Gainsborough shows that John Chapman, a veterinary surgeon aged 36, lived in Spittal Terrace, Gainsborough, with his wife, Jane, aged 32, and children, John aged 10, Mary 8, Henry 6, Charles 4, William 3, Edward 1, together with Mary Clarke aged 62, described as a widow and late innkeeper, plus two servants.

Looking at the birthplaces of John Chapman's children, William was born in West Bridgford in 1847/48, presumably at the Trent Bridge Inn, whilst Edward was born in Gainsborough in 1849/50. All the earlier children were born in St Mary's Parish in Nottingham. This provides evidence that John Chapman and family had lived in Nottingham, but moved back to the Trent Bridge Inn shortly after William Clarke left for London. The birth of Edward, in either 1849 or 1850, confirms the earlier suggestion that John Chapman had indeed left the Trent Bridge Inn for Gainsborough in the 1849/50 period. The other revealing point contained in the census entry is that Mary Clarke describes herself as a 'widow' which, as we have said, is odd when her husband is the best known cricketer in the British Isles and touring the whole of England during 1851. I believe it is safe to assume that William Clarke's absence from the All-England Eleven v Gainsborough was purely diplomatic – the next match he missed was in mid-September due to a very serious injury. The 1852 edition of *Lillywhite's Guide* gives Mr Chapman as the proprietor of the Trent Bridge Cricket Ground, but I would suggest that this is merely a reprint from the 1850 edition, having not been updated.

The MCC agreed to play Clarke's England Eleven at Lord's, the home side being allowed fourteen players. According to Haygarth, it was the only time MCC fielded more than eleven players against another Eleven. The match ended in an acrimonious row. There had been a great deal of betting on the outcome. Caffyn and Box were batting in the AEE's second innings, the score being 114 for five. AEE required one run to win, when MCC ordered the drawing of stumps, it being the agreed time to end the match. MCC were acting strictly to the Law, but Haygarth (who played in the match and made the highest score for MCC) commented, 'it was certainly not cricket or sportsmanlike'. There was uproar at the time and one wonders if this niggled rather with William Clarke, whose relationship with Lord's and MCC was to break down the following season.

With so many more AEE matches in 1851, Clarke found it necessary to recruit four additional professionals, Julius Caesar, George Anderson, James Grundy and Daniel Day. The first two were to remain with All-England until after Clarke's death, but Day played only in 1851, whilst Grundy ceded to the United during 1852. A biography of Julius Caesar, written by Geoff Amey, was published in 2000 and tells of the life and

The hard graft. The All-England Eleven travelling from Spalding, completing the last stage of their journey from Salford, to play a Twenty-Two of Wisbech over three days in June 1851. Clarke opened the batting in both AEE innings and took fifteen wickets.

tragic last years of Caesar, who died aged 47 in 1878. Richard Daft in *Kings of Cricket* describes Caesar as 'one of the smartest men altogether I ever came across. ... His hitting was as smart and clean as anything that could be witnessed.' Caesar played for his native county of Surrey from 1849 to 1867.

George Anderson, the Yorkshire batsman from Bedale, is one of the cricketers who feature in *Old English Cricketers* by Old Ebor, published in 1900. Anderson states that William Clarke used to come up to Bedale to coach the young players and also laid out the Bedale cricket ground. Anderson relates two Clarke stories:

> Life in the All-England Eleven was very jolly and I often look back upon those days with pleasant feelings. Old Clarke, our General, as we called him, was a very dry customer. I remember one gay young spark telling him he wished to learn cricketing, and asked what was the first thing to do. 'Get your finger nails cut,' was the laconic reply. On another occasion a lady asked Clarke's advice about her son. She thought he would make an excellent cricketer, as he 'stood six feet in his stockings'. 'Dear me, what a large number of toes he must have,' was the dry, if not polite, comment by which Clarke crushed the maternal feelings.

Anderson states in the same piece that he was paid £5 a match, or up to £6 for long journeys, but that after expenses there was not much left. In view of later comments on the misery that Clarke supposedly caused his players, Anderson's memories of how he enjoyed travelling with Clarke and the AEE provides another version of the atmosphere and general bonhomie. Anderson played intermittently for Yorkshire from 1850 to 1869 and went with Parr's team to Australia and New Zealand in 1863/64. He died at Bedale in North Yorkshire in 1902.

James 'Jemmy' Grundy (1824-1873) was born in Radford, Nottingham and was engaged in Norfolk for four years before he joined the MCC groundstaff in 1851. In the same year he made his Notts debut and proved an excellent all-rounder, both for MCC and the county. Caffyn notes: 'He was exceedingly good company and always ready with a song when called upon.' He fell out with Clarke, but the reason doesn't seem to be recorded.

The fourth new professional, Daniel Day, ran the cricket ground at Itchen, Southampton though he was born in Surrey in 1807 and played in some matches for his native county. He turned out in only nine AEE matches, all in the 1851 season.

Apart from the presence of Mynn and Felix, Clarke did not incorporate any amateurs into his side, except for the very occasional match. His son, Alfred, played in two AEE games during the season and became a permanent fixture during 1852. He was 20 on his debut and was considered a useful batsman and good outfield; later he acted as the person who organized the travel arrangements for the Eleven.

Clarke appeared in the two Gentlemen v Players matches at Lord's in 1851 as well as the two North v South matches – he selected the North side on both occasions. The Surrey v Nottinghamshire match at The Oval duly took place as advertised – the first time the two counties had ever met. It is perhaps worth listing the Notts players: William Clarke (capt), F.Tinley, Joe Guy, George Parr, Butler Parr, James Grundy, Samuel Parr, Charles Brown, George Butler, Thomas Nixon and Alfred Clarke. The Nottinghamshire umpire was Thomas Barker; R.C.Tinley was selected but unable to come, Alfred Clarke taking his place. Surrey won by 75 runs, Notts having collapsed to Daniel Day (seven for 22) in their first innings.

On 11 September 1851 the All-England Eleven began a match at Newburgh Park, the ground of Sir George Wombwell, third baronet, near Ampleforth in North Yorkshire. England scored 144: Newburgh Park were dismissed for 79, with Clarke (ten for 49) and Wisden (nine for 27) bowling unchanged. Clarke bowled 30 overs, Wisden 29. England collapsed in their second innings, all out 29. Clarke and Wisden then began to demolish the home side in the second innings. Clarke had taken a further nine wickets and had begun his 33rd over when, in throwing a ball to Tom Box, the wicketkeeper, he seriously damaged his shoulder and had to retire from the match – England went on to win by 11 runs. He was unable to play in the next four matches, but *As Centuries Blend*, the history of Clydesdale C.C. on whose home ground the AEE met Scotland on 18, 19 and 20 September, notes:

> One disappointment was the absence from the England team of the masterful William Clarke; but he did his best to make up for that. He was indefatigable in circling the ground, explaining the game. If Clarke had played, the crowd might have seen something of the captaincy of which he was said to be capable.

He re-appeared as an umpire at Teignbridge on 29 September and then played purely as a batsman in the last fixture of the season at Hove v Sixteen of Sussex. Fred Lillywhite in his 1852 *Guide* wrote: 'It is a painful duty to record that he [Clarke] broke his shoulder bone which, at the time of writing this, it is thought will disable him from again lending his valuable assistance in the field.'

Fortunately the injury was not as severe as Lillywhite surmised and Clarke certainly proved that by bowling unchanged through the first innings of the first AEE match of 1852, delivering 49.2 overs and taking 12 wickets!

Clarke took 84 wickets in first-class matches in the 1851 season, the most in his career. Some idea of William Clarke's reputation in the cricket world in 1851 is demonstrated by the inclusion in a book *Cricket Notes* by William Bolland, President of I Zingari, and issued that season, of a final chapter by William Clark [sic]. This chapter is integral to the understanding of the famous cricketer and is reprinted in an Appendix to this volume. Simultaneously, *The Cricket Field*, by James Pycroft, was published. Like Nyren's book, 'Pycroft' ran through a number of editions. Chapter IX of the original is entitled 'Bowling – An Hour With Old Clarke' and tends to follow the same message as Clarke's chapter in Bolland's book. Pycroft's remarks are set out in full on page 77, above.

The two pieces in Bolland and Pycroft demonstrate just how important William Clarke was as a player and a captain in the early 1850s. This standing among the intelligentsia of the game was reinforced the following year, when Nicholas Felix published, perhaps in answer to Clarke's Bolland essay, *How To Play Clarke,* subtitled 'being an attempt to Unravel the Mysteries of the Ball and to show What Defence and Hitting are to be Employed Against this Celebrated Bowler.' This short work is also illustrated by Felix. He was a man with a good sense of humour and fond of using word play to comical advantage, though Clarke sometimes trumped him. Felix related the following incident when a train in which Clarke and Felix were travelling stopped unexpectedly with a view of a cricket match seen out of the window:

'Did you see that, Muster Felix?' remarked Clarke.

'I did.'

'Whoey, then that's juist as folk ought to play me.'

'How is that?'

'Whoey, with the head,' responded Clarke.

The poor batsman had just received a ball straight on his head.

Chapter Nine

Controversy

'At a meeting held at the Adelphi Hotel, Sheffield, this 7th day of September, 1852, by the members of the United Eleven of England, it was unanimously resolved, That neither the members of the above Eleven shall at any time play in any cricket match, for or against, wherein William Clarke may have the management or control (county matches excepted), in consequence of the treatment they have received from him at Newmarket and elsewhere.

John Wisden, James Dean, Thomas Adams, Thomas Hunt, George Grainger Brown, John Lillywhite, Thomas Nixon, George Picknell, Samuel Dakin, George Chatterton, Thomas Lockyer, James Grundy, Thomas Sherman, Henry Wright.'

Exactly what happened at Newmarket seems never to have been revealed. To go back a month or two, John Wisden and James Dean had decided between themselves to set up a rival to Clarke's All-England Eleven. Both were Sussex professionals. Wisden himself had played in 31 of the 34 AEE matches in 1851, including all the last batch of games. In 1852 he became the professional coach at Harrow School and, whilst he and Parr still were lessees of the ground in Leamington, it doesn't seem certain that he continued to live in that town. As a resident he had played for North v South, but in 1852 he appeared for South v North at The Oval on 1 and 2 July. He continued to take part in the few Sussex matches of the season. His co-conspirator, Dean, was a ground bowler at Lord's from 1837 to 1861; and although he played in the All-England Eleven in its early days, he (apart from two matches) was not seen in Clarke's side after 1848.

On 26, 27 and 28 August 1852 the All-England Eleven played on the new ground at Hereford Racecourse, whilst on the same dates, Wisden and Dean staged their first United All-England Eleven match on Day's Ground at Itchen versus Twenty Gentlemen of Hampshire. Two of Clarke's team from the match at Teignbridge earlier in the week, Thomas Adams and James Grundy, deserted Clarke for the Wisden/Dean combination. Neither could be described as integral parts of Clarke's side. Adams had not played for the AEE in any games in 1851 and Grundy, although making his AEE debut in 1851, appeared in only ten of the 34 matches. As Professor West states in his book *The Elevens of England,* the impression given by some historians that Clarke treated most of his players so callously that they moved almost en bloc into the Wisden/Dean camp is clearly a misconception. Aside from Grundy, Adams, Wisden and Dean, of the other nine original members of the United Eleven, *viz* Lockyer, Chatterton, Wright, Sampson, G.G.Brown, John Lillywhite, F.P.Miller, Picknell and Nixon, only Chatterton had much connection to the AEE and he ceased to play, save in three matches, after 1850.

The two England teams then played on 30, 31 August and 1 September. The AEE engagement was at Ilkeston, the United at Newmarket. Clarke did not go to Ilkeston but travelled to Newmarket and clearly told Wisden and Dean what he thought of them, hence the grand announcement at Sheffield on 7 September.

The United Eleven played only four matches in 1852, whereas Clarke staged 26. The depth of feeling between the main promoters of the two England Elevens was to emerge in the columns of the sporting newspaper *Bell's Life* during December, but before going forward to that acrimonious correspondence, the other significant events of the 1852 season need recording.

Scores and Biographies begins its coverage of the 1852 season with a cricket song for The Eleven of England. The final verse runs:

> Then long may 'Old Clarke' be up to the mark,
> And guide us to triumphs again;
> We never shall see better leader than he,
> We may look for his like in vain.
> > Come join in the toast,
> > 'Tis a glorious boast,
> All classes may share in its joys;
> > Both peasant and peer
> > Find ecstacy here,
> Then Cricket for ever my boys
> Then Cricket for ever my boys.

This chapter began with the events of late summer, but to put matters in sequence it is necessary to return to the start of the 1852 season. The AEE side played five matches beginning on 10 May. In the game at Hyde Park, Sheffield against Fourteen of Yorkshire, Clarke took eight for 80 in the first innings and nine for 80 in the second. After the five matches Clarke appeared successively for England at Lord's and for Surrey v England at The Oval. There were five more AEE matches, including the two between 14 and 19 June. The first of these was at King's Lynn from which town the All-England Eleven had to travel across the fens by stage coach to play at Sleaford the following days. This journey was described by several players, the coach getting lost in the dark and Martingell lighting a flare to read a signpost in order to ascertain the correct route. Felix sketched a picture of the 'lost' coach.

Several additional eleven-a-side games took place at The Oval and Lord's, ending in Gentlemen v Players at Lord's, with Dean and Wisden opening the Players' innings and Clarke batting at No.11. One wonders whether Clarke was aware of the Wisden/Dean plans at that juncture – the game ended on 21 July.

When the AEE went to Northampton on 12 August, Wisden and Dean were given men for the Northampton side. The following week Clarke, Dean and Wisden played for the MCC-selected England team v Kent at Canterbury

*More hard graft. The well-known sketch by Nathaniel Felix showing
William Martingell climbing a Fenland signpost at dead of night to find the way.*

– the appearance of the United England team was just eight days away.

On 2 September, Clarke reappeared at Trent Bridge, after a gap of six complete seasons, in Nottinghamshire v Surrey. The *Nottingham Review* comments: 'This match was entirely brought about by the indefatigable exertions of the well-known Charley Brown,' the Nottinghamshire wicketkeeper, though on 23 July the same paper had reported: 'We have the pleasure of informing our readers that after much expense of time and trouble, the Committee of the Nottingham Town and County Cricket Club have succeeded in arranging for a return match against Surrey at Trent Bridge.'

It is believed that the Trent Bridge Inn and Ground had been run by a Mr Wildey, following John Chapman's move to Gainsborough, but the 1851 census gives only two servants living at the Inn on the day the count was made. Joseph Hickling, a much more renowned landlord, took over the lease later in the 1850s. Matches played by both Nottingham Commercial and Notts Amateurs at Trent Bridge are published in the press during the season.

Despite the desertion of the AEE by two professionals, the only new recruit to the side to make regular appearances in 1852 was John Bickley, a fast round-arm bowler who had played in some Nottinghamshire matches since 1847. He came from Keyworth and was a notable all-round athlete.

The whole of the rift between Clarke and the deserters led by Wisden and Dean blew up afresh in the columns of the major sporting paper of the day, *Bell's Life,* on 4 December 1852. The editor had clearly thought long and hard before deciding to publish – the letter is dated 4 November – and actually states that the piece had been published following several weeks' delay.

The missive was headed: NOTES ON CRICKET: OR, DOINGS OF THE PAST SEASON.

The writer began by describing matches played by MCC and at Lord's, then at The Oval, together with other games, before he launched what amounts to an attack on Clarke and the All-England Eleven:

> For the country matches I must dwell upon a party *calling themselves* 'The Eleven of England.' Is this to be understood as the *best eleven cricketers in England,* or a title by which they distinguish themselves from others? I should imagine, judging from the merits of the men, that the latter was the case; and, to prevent the public (in the 'far North' especially) from being 'gulled', I shall give some 'doings' of the 'so-called Eleven of England', which, by assistance, I have managed to collect. It is evident people go under the impression that they are going to see '*the picked men of England!*' Whom do they see for them? Why, such men as *Mynn, Hillyer, A.Clarke, W.Clarke and A.Marshall,* in addition to what may be termed 'good old ones' such as Guy, Box, Felix. This, indeed, is a weak party, and the secretary of it takes great care that their *opponents* shall be as weak, for he frequently, I am told, objects to professionals *playing against him,* otherwise it would be impossible with such a 'team' to have won the matches they have already done this season. How is it you do not play with the eleven at 'so and so?' is frequently asked of professionals. The answer would be, 'Clarke objected to me.' Why does he do so? 'Because he has a weak party himself.' Why has he a weak party himself is then immediately inquired? 'Because he has power and badly uses it.' This I will explain. Five years ago Clarke introduced these matches in the north of England, and had the entire management himself, whereby he pocketed a considerable amount of money each match. A party of cricketers then signed their names at Brighton *not to play for him again,* as he acted improperly. To get out of this trouble he proposed a committee (and made himself secretary), which was formed at Lord's and ran as follows: Clarke, sec., Felix, treasurer, Hillyer, F.Pilch, A.Mynn. Box was afterwards made one. I hear this season Parr has been substituted for Pilch, the latter not *exactly understanding* how affairs were managed. Although there is *at present* this committee, they have nothing whatever to do with selecting players (they however do not do it) or the arrangements in any way. Thus if a match was wanted by a country club, Clarke must have been applied to, who (with perhaps one or two exceptions) never plays matches for less than £66 (unless for a well-known player, or playing matches at *a very short distance,* and in many places will get £70 and has, I believe, got £75.) This is a bargain made by himself, and he *receives* and *pays* all (the latter not until some months have elapsed after the season is over), so that it can easily be imagined why such an eleven travel the country, Clarke receives the amount for 'first-rate players' and pays it partly to 'second-rate ones'. Thus it may be said, he obtains money under an 'equivocal state of

things'. His lowest sum, as I have above stated, for a match is in almost every case, £66. He pays as follows, as near as possible: Felix, I will say, about £6, Parr £5, Martingell £5, Box £5, Caffyn £4 10s, Caesar £4 10s, Guy £5 (doubtful if so much), Anderson £4, Bickley £5, Mynn £5, the umpire £4, the scorer £1 10s – total £54 10s. Clarke, therefore, to account for the £66, pockets for himself £11 10s every match!! and if he gets £70, the additional sum is added. If *a gentleman or his son played* (which they often did), *still extra money fell to him.* Hence A.Marshall, Esq., and A.Clarke playing so often. This is a cause of such an eleven travelling under the title of 'The Eleven of England'. Wisden, one of the finest bowlers we have, left him, owing to unfair treatment. Martingell and Fuller Pilch have done the same. I am informed he has extra money for a long distance, such as going into Scotland; the players, however, receive *no extra pay whatever.* The committee, I think, Mr Editor, should have the power of using the balance money, and pay the secretary and treasurer what they think proper for their services. They should also have the power of *selecting the players*, and we then would see less drawn matches and much more good cricket. Clarke, it appears to me, has secured more power than he possessed previous to the formation of the committee; he not only *plays* whom he pleases, but prevents whom he pleases *from playing against him.* This has caused a party of cricketers to act in the same way towards him, as was done about five years ago at Brighton; only, I believe, in this case, they have signed not to play *against him* anywhere, as well as *with him.* I have been favoured with the names; they are as follows: Dean, Wisden, Chatterton, Grundy, John Lillywhite, Adams, Hunt, Wright, Nixon, George Brown, Picknell, Sherman, Lockyer, and others have signified their intentions in a similar manner. I, myself, cannot see but that they are justly right in so acting, especially after the most *Insulting* letter, sent to Newmarket in connection with the 'United Eleven', which is formed of the above players. The letter was shown to me while there, by a gentleman connected with the club, which accuses them of using *his name, &c,* in the placards, and doubts whether the party (meaning the 'United Eleven') will make their appearance on the day named. If I had been in the place of Dean and Wisden, Mr Editor, I should have kindly asked you to have inserted it, leaving the public to judge therefrom.

I have frequently met the 'Eleven of Eleven' and have no doubt that their matches (as far as they can do so) are played honourably, and they win if they can. A friend of mine, however, while at Newcastle, informed me shortly after the match had taken place, that England might have won the match easily. This has just come to my recollection; he said there was *an hour and a half lost one day because the proprietor wished it,* as the game was proceeding too fast. This *was allowed, and when the stumps were drawn six runs were wanted to win.* My friend also informed me that he had heard one of the players (who had been at the wicket) say, 'If he had *known* the game was so close, he and his partner could *have won it.'* So that, Mr Editor, there must be a 'lack of interest' for, either the party who was at the wicket ought to have made the inquiry, or those connected with the 'in' side should have had the fact communicated to them. Fancy for one moment two country clubs contending together; the first innings decides which are the victors; the time for drawing (as agreed) is half-past five; three minutes is wanted and six runs also. *Would not the two batsmen know it?* Such was the case at Newcastle.

The Hereford match, where the Eleven were also engaged, I am sorry to be obliged to acknowledge, I lost seven pounds in going to see. I did not, however, stop; for when I bought a card, I perceived the following *Eleven for England* had nearly completed their innings: Caesar, Grundy, Anderson, Parr, Caffyn, Guy, *A.Clarke, A.Mynn*, W.Clarke, Bickley and Hillyer. The latter, when I entered the ground, was just called from the duties of 'umpireship' to play in the room of Box, for whom Caffyn *kept wicket*. Neither of those I have marked in italics are capable, Mr Editor, of playing for England. Much dissatisfaction was the result, the county being young as cricketers, it was likely to do very great injury; £70, I believe, was collected for the Eleven, which, with their own *professionals* and additional expenses, was principally got together by crowns, half-crowns, shillings &c. This will convince the reader how popular the game of cricket is likely to become in Herefordshire, if not prevented by the introduction of men who have no pretensions to cricket, and players whose days have gone by. I should strongly advise clubs to know and be certain what sort of an eleven they are engaging to show them cricket. I have dwelt very long on this subject, Mr Editor, but these "doings" are totally injurious to the noble and manly game of cricket, and I am confident your cricketing readers will thank you for the insertion in your widely circulating journal of that which tends to promote the game. What expense it has been to me to procure the above information will be well expended by the satisfaction of knowing that our provincial cricketers may realize great benefit from it, and also that it may be the means of the game being played as it should be. The above parties played 30 matches, of which 11 were drawn, 10 won and 4 lost. The "United Eleven of England" are, it appears to me, established on a far better principle and have connected with them most of the *best cricketers*. They played four matches, won three and drawn one; they were on two occasions very weak. If they wish for good matches they must play their strength; include no gentleman unless he be really worthy of a place. They have on their side most of the 'skill' of the country, and conducted on honest principles, which appears to be the fact, they must succeed ...

Cambridge, November 4   A Lover of Cricket.

It was in *The Era* of 26 December 1852, that Clarke's response to 'A Lover of Cricket' appeared:

If I had taken the advice of my friends and some of the leading members of the Marylebone Committee, I should not have answered this 'Lover of Cricket', but as the article in question is principally directed against me with a *leetle* colouring, I thought I had a duty to perform to myself and the public to expose the malicious fabrications of this impartial lover of cricket.

The best armour against injustice is a proper degree of spirit to repel the wrongs that are done or designed against us; but if we divest ourselves of all resentment, we shall prove too irresolute both in resisting the attacks of injustice and inflicting punishment upon those who have committed it; we shall therefore sink into contempt, and by the tameness of our spirit invoke the malicious to abuse and affront us.

When all the gentlemen and secretaries whom I have the honour to correspond and match with, and the committee I have the pleasure to act with, are perfectly satisfied with my arrangements, both as regards players, moneys paid and received – *and it is by the management of the money that cricket is introduced into districts it never would have been* – I say, when they are satisfied, what occasion have I to reply to the long rigmarole of fabrications and *sheer nonsense* that only shows the utter ignorance of the subject that he is writing about. I know his name to be not *Sorrywether* but something like it, portly *barrister, noted* for his *old Dando qualifications* and his expensive professionals, old Dean and old Lilly, who cost about two penny postage stamps. To his assertion of Pilch's withdrawal –

From Pilch – 'Dear Clarke – In reply to yours, I am not aware of ever drawing my name from your committee, and I am very sure I never told anyone so. I had not read the long, sickly, childish prattle till after I received yours, &c &c.'

Wisden and I did not part on money matters, but quite a different subject.

He is only right in three names of money given for playing. Suppose him to be right in those that are engaged at a fixed salary, they are paid according to agreement. They run no risk. I originated these matches, and my time is wholly devoted in the winter to making and arranging them. I had a 400 or 500 miles' journey, a month since, to look at two new grounds where we are going to play, and where we have not been. I have been since last season in correspondence with sixty or seventy places and when I have settled as to places I have to begin again to fix the time &c, &c.

Does this impartial lover suppose I or any other man would give his time, his trouble, his expense, his ingenuity, and risk and have no prospect of a return? Just like all the other *childish prattle!* Does the manager of a theatre, after he has paid the salary agreed upon, divide the receipts, of any? If such a doctrine as that is to be put forth there will be something *'looming in the future'!*

A.Clarke did *not receive* the money for playing at Kelso, but the person he played for, who is ill. It was no benefit A.Marshall, Esq., going round with us; the same number went round as if he had not gone, but we are fond of him, and I hope he will go with us again. We began 1846 with one gentleman, and one ever since at times. He says the committee never interferes. If that were *true*, what a *great compliment to me,* and it is by the management of the funds that cricket is introduced into districts it never would have been, making 180 matches.

I had been applied to from *Newmarket and Salisbury,* and could not go. Playing at The Oval, I was informed *(I gave them my author)* that Pilch and my name were in the bills going to play at Newmarket. I wrote to Newmarket to say they might play whom they liked, but they must not use the All England Eleven names to deceive the public. It appears the secretary at Newmarket is named Clarke, so it answered two purposes; they could take it for which they liked. If they stand so high, why use the names of the not fit-to-play party? For Pilch's name was there, but finding by being rejected by the gentlemen of Wiltshire they did not stand so high with the public as they did with themselves, as was proved by the miserable thin attendance they had at the two or three places they went to, they adopted those means.

This lover wishes it to be understood that A.Clarke, A.Mynn, A.Marshall, Esq., and Hillyer play in all the matches. Now, in looking over the England score book, I find that in 24 matches out of 28 the Eleven consisted of the following: N.Felix, A.Mynn, Box, Clarke, Parr, Guy, Caffyn, Caesar, Anderson, Bickley and Martingell, with sometimes, Grundy and Adams, for those unavoidably absent. Aye! Bickley. He is the best short slip that ever *played at cricket,* and see his *averages of bowling.* Now for A.Mynn. Nine places out of ten I am written to request him to come. He has played in 15 matches out of 28, *instead of all the matches* – had 26 innings, scored 297 runs, averaged 11 and 11 over. Martingell played in 18 matches, got 132 runs, average 4 and 4 over. So you see the *bad* player gets 16 a match more than Martingell, and we must not say much about the difference in fielding.

With regard the signing, it's a rope of sand. But I think they have left out the talent of bowling. Where are the Tinleys, Jacksons, Berrys, Armitages, Crosslands, Divers, Buttresses, Arnolds, Joys and others? Look at their performances; they could not get them in the snare, for they knew what I had been the means of doing for them. Look at Wisden and Dean, at Northampton, with four or five of the most noted from Rugby, and twenty-two at their back, best almost at one innings, the All England getting about 125 from those renowned bowlers, whilst those most noted were about all ciphered by the bowlers not fit. Look again at Nixon – at Ipswich he gets one wicket against us, and at Newton Abbot the same number – rather a long journey (400 miles) I take it, for one wicket.

How is it this gifted party that is established on such perfect principles are spectators, whilst the not-fit-to-play party are all engaged at Lord's and Canterbury? After the Surrey and England match at Lord's, I take Nottingham under my *own* management – mind you, under my own management – and beat Surrey at one innings, and 43 runs to spare, *the same party that had beaten England, but I did not play Nixon,* getting 6 wickets, Bickley 2, and 2 run out. By the fielding of A.Clarke the first innings, got 6 wickets, Bickley 2 and Grundy 2. The second innings they got 138 runs. They got 65 runs from me at both innings and I got 12 wickets. *'Oh no, he never mentions it!'* Let this one-sided gentleman add the following two matches played in London to the other five he picked out that I and Grundy played in, I think that will open the eyes of the readers to his impartiality:

	M	Balls	Runs	Wkts	Av.p.M	Av.R	Av
Clarke	2	516	154	38	10	77	4
Grundy	2	216	69	6	3	38	10

I was told not to bring Dean three years ago, they did not want to see such cricket as that – *good judges too* – Now that is one that would come at any price and give me the sayings and doings of his brother cricketers in at the bargain. This 'Lover' says that in the year '51 at The Oval, there were the two strongest Elevens ever got together. The broken-down *Hillyer* played. Wisden went back to his own side, the South: he was to turn the scale. I won again, by 60 runs. The first innings I got 7 wickets, Buttress 1, two run out; second innings, I got 8 wickets, Buttress 2. They got 96 runs from me out of 213. I got 15 wickets. Grundy bowled in that match. *Oh, no, he never mentions it!*

Wisden got one wicket on the South side. Kent and England at Canterbury, none: Surrey and Sussex at Brighton, 2 wickets. But look at the quantity of runs at one innings each; they got 500 runs, there must have been something wrong; and this terrible match at Lord's, he gets 2 wickets in the match and they get 55 runs. I got 3 wickets, they got 90, my average 30, his 27.5 – wonderful difference. I have been on the winning side of the North and South matches for these last six years. I won every match in London, year '51, but two and had won sixteen out of eighteen, when an accident put a stop to my career; and this year I should have been on the winning side in 25 out of 32 matches if they had been played out.

Look at the records of matches where I have played. I got all the wickets (15) at Brighton two years since; Wisden, Martingell and Hillyer at the other end. There is something belonging to cricket besides bowling, and batting and fielding – you may as well call my friend, Jonathan Kentfield, the finest billiard player in England, a dodger, because he plays the game with science.

Cricketer's Guide says: 'Clarke is a *remarkably* fine slow bowler, and his precision and thorough knowledge of the game is *wonderful*. He is the able Secretary of the All England Eleven, and arranges all their matches, which is a task of great labour. He has done much to promote the game of Cricket throughout England and Scotland.'

Look at such men as Parr, Caffyn, Caesar, Anderson, Bickley; Box at the wicket, Guy at the stop. Why, I would go a hundred miles any day to see them field. For the character of our Eleven *vide* Lord Eglinton's speech at Glasgow, in 1851. F.Bailey, Esq., at Kelso, in proposing the health of the Eleven this year said, 'I need say very little in regard to them. They are too well known to all of you. It is well known that in almost innumerable multitudes of matches in which they have been engaged for several years past they have invariably so conducted themselves as to have gained the highest character for honour, straightforward dealing and integrity, that any body of public characters ever possessed in Great Britain.'

We shall not alter. I should not have been so personal, but this is got up by a party at the back of the United, and they are made the tools, through which means they think to break up the All England Eleven. It will all prove useless, for their foundation is built upon a rock, and will take as much to break it down as it would the Tubular Bridge, for it is too firmly established.

I have been the means of taking the best players – ay, the best players – and other connected with them, *renowned for cricket*, such as a Pilch, a Felix, a Mynn, a Box, a Parr &c., to every man's door in England and Scotland – and, if I live and am well, in Ireland and in the heart of Wales next year; which, if it had not been for me, the majority of the people in those countries would never have seen such cricketers.

I have been the means of bringing some of the best players from distant counties for *Londoners* to see them they had heard of, that if it had not been for me would have remained in obscurity in the hedge rows and bye lanes of England.

I have been good enough to be Daguerreotyped for the frontispiece of 'The Cricket Field'. I have been thought good enough to take me in oil-painting to be put in the Pavilion at Lord's. I have been thought good enough to ask my opinion about the merits of players when they were going to choose them for the great matches at Lord's – not only good enough for that, but they knew they should have it honestly – and been thought good enough to manage the field with the best elevens. And to conclude, to show the estimation we are held in, we are engaged in forty-two matches for the next season of 1853, beginning at Lincoln on the 4th of May; then for Ireland and Scotland, and play our way back to the Southern and Western parts of England, and shall be playing every day till the 30th of September. We play in ten new districts, and all our matches will be conducted on the *same principles* as they have hitherto been – honour, honesty, good feeling, and good conduct. Wherever there is new talent that is worth changing, it will be brought out. I am now *thought good enough* for Nottingham to ask to play Nottingham against all England at Lord's. I am *now thought good enough* for Nottingham to ask me for Nottingham to play Sussex, or any other eleven, provided *I will play* (mark that, you impartial 'Lover of Cricket'!), bar Surrey and Yorkshire. Because they would cause no interest, having beaten Surrey; and I am now thought good enough by such players as Felix (President), Mynn, Pilch, Box, Parr, Hillyer, the committee, to manage, and play, and be *the* All England bowler.

W.Clarke
Secretary to the All England Cricket Committee
Anglesea Hotel, 22 December

There were five or six other letters in *The Era*, either supporting or not, Clarke and his management of the All-England Eleven. Alfred Mynn's brother was perhaps the most notable of Clarke's supporters and his letter was republished in Patrick Morrah's biography of Alfred Mynn. For the purposes of this present book, the two principal letters will suffice. In *The Elevens of England,* Professor West states that 'A Lover of Cricket' was Charles George Merewether, QC (1823-1884), Conservative MP for Northampton from 1874 to 1880. James Pycroft acknowledges Merewether's assistance in the preface to *The Cricket Field.*

The finer points of the argument. William Clarke and Charles Merewether conducted their dispute in these tight-packed columns of Bell's Life, left and The Era, right, in December 1852.

It will have been noticed that Clarke, in his letter, quotes extensively his bowling performances achieved during the year. Today's cricket statisticians will, perhaps, be surprised that cricket stats meant so much to players as far back as in 1852. This point, however, is further emphasized in December 1852 with the following note in *Bell's Life:*

> Clarke's Averages: By an unfortunate, but unintentional mistake, Clarke's averages were wrongly given in our list [of leading players' records for 1852]. Clarke informs us that instead of 31 matches, 306 wickets, it should have been 31 matches, 440 wickets.

When the 1853 summer came round, the professional cricketers in both the All-England and United All-England teams were probably relieved to return to the playing field, and try to forget Mr Merewether and the series of abusive letters his original attack on Clarke provoked.

Those spectators going to watch the All-England Eleven, however, would miss the familiar face of Nicholas Felix – rheumatism prevented him from playing, though he did make two appearances in late August, his final game being at Torquay v Twenty-Two of Devonshire. Whether or not he continued in his role as President of the All-England Eleven doesn't seem to be recorded. William Martingell also left Clarke's eleven, possibly by mutual consent after his caustic comments relating to Clarke in the press. Fuller Pilch also did not play in 1853, the Kent batsman having made just two outings in 1852. The two newcomers were Sam Parr, George's brother and a practical joker, and Charles Arnold. A fast round-arm bowler, Arnold began his professional career with Bury St Edmunds aged 20 in 1842, although he was born and always lived in Cambridge. He stayed with the AEE just one summer, but Sam Parr would remain for years to come, much to the irritation of some of his fellow players, as Daft notes in *Kings of Cricket*.

The first match of 1853 was at St Helens in Lancashire against the local twenty-two, but a week later came one of the most important matches ever played by Nottinghamshire – versus England at Lord's. *Lillywhite's Guide* comments that 'The ground was attended by a great number of the aristocracy. The representatives of England were selected by Lord Charles Russell and were under the able management of W.Nicholson, Esq, while the county was guided by the experience of the Hon F.Ponsonby.' The England team was thoroughly representative and included both Dean and Wisden. Clarke took eight wickets as did John Bickley; George Parr made the game's highest score of 49, with Nottinghamshire winning by 27 runs. This victory resulted in Nottinghamshire being acclaimed the Champion County. Ponsonby later became the sixth Earl of Bessborough; he had played for Harrow and Cambridge and was a founding member of I Zingari. Clarke's *Practical Hints* are dedicated to Ponsonby but the latter does not seem to be connected in any way directly to Nottinghamshire cricket. The *Guide* which covers the 1853 season states that Nottinghamshire County Cricket Club have C.Thornton as honorary secretary and J.Johnson as treasurer. It seems that Charley Brown had shamed the 'gentlemen of Nottingham' into putting the county club on a more stable footing!

There followed seven successive All-England matches – lost three, won two, drawn two. The twenty-twos almost always had given men – three of the seven sides actually had three given men each. Clarke then played in the MCC-selected England team v Kent at Lord's. Dean and several United Eleven men were also in the England side, but a fortnight later, when the North v South match was staged at The Oval, all the United players refused to represent their respective sides, because the match had been organized by Clarke. The same state of affairs applied when England opposed a combined Kent and Sussex eleven at Tunbridge Wells later that July. However, when England played their traditional fixture v Kent as part of the Canterbury festival, Clarke and Wisden, supposedly arch-enemies, bowled together unchanged through both Kent innings.

An early photograph of Alfred Clarke, who played 55 first-class matches between 1851 and 1864.

The 1854 season began much more slowly than the summers immediately preceding it. There was an early practice game at Trent Bridge, commencing 17 April, when Players of Nottinghamshire opposed the Gentlemen with five players. Alfred Clarke appeared, George Parr hit a century for the Gentlemen and the attendance was reported as good, but there was no sign of Old Clarke. He did not appear in any match for another month and then it was in the first AEE fixture of the season at Upton Park in south-west Essex (now West Ham) on 23, 24 and 25 May. Clarke took 13 wickets in Upton Park's second innings. The United Eleven's season had begun earlier and two games completed prior to the AEE arrival in Essex.

After their success in 1853, Nottinghamshire opposed England at Lord's on 5 and 6 June. Nottinghamshire lost but the match was more memorable for the row caused by Clarke. Fred Lillywhite describes what happened:

> An unusual occurrence took place in this match, respecting a 'run out'. The new law now tells the batsman to obtain permission of their opponents before they can be allowed a substitute, which was done, Buttress acting for Caesar; the latter, however, drove a ball forward from Clarke, and immediately ran and made the run, the *substitute* remaining on his ground. The 'Old General' [Clarke] knowing *some one* ought to be out, put the wicket down at the end Caesar had made, and appealed to the Umpire, who gave him 'not out'; but, however, contrary to the Laws of Cricket, Clarke proceeded to the pavilion, to ask the opinion of the gentlemen, who, after a lapse of time, came to the determination that Caesar, having left his wicket wrongfully, should be given out. But nevertheless, according to the law on the subject, Wisden was the party who left, and was *away* from the wicket that was put down. At all events, the Umpire's decision should not have been disputed by Clarke, whether wrong or right.

There followed four All-England matches in succession, after which Surrey came to Trent Bridge to play Nottinghamshire. In the press George Parr and Julius Caesar were given as the organizers, and it was stated that 'though but short notice was given to the manager of the Trent Bridge ground, it was got into good order.' One assumes that Clarke was not used as a promoter because members of the United Eleven would not then appear. Three United men, Lockyer, Sherman and Grundy, took part in their respective county elevens. Be that as it may, Surrey won with ease. William Clarke took 12 Surrey wickets, including eight in the second innings, but Notts could not retrieve their first-innings deficit of 75 runs.

On 17 and 18 July the Gentlemen opposed the Players at Lord's. Clarke and his All-England men refused the invitation to take part. Clarke had, either deliberately or by accident, arranged for All-England to play an eighteen of Maidstone on the same dates as the Lord's match. The MCC took umbrage at Clarke effectively snubbing the Club and resolved that never again would Clarke be invited to play at Lord's. Clarke's reaction was to instruct the players he controlled never to accept an invitation to appear at Lord's again. Therefore at the end of July when a match was arranged MCC v England, no All-England man turned out, but on the same dates, the AEE opposed Twenty-Two of Bingham.

Cricket now had a double dispute on its hands – Clarke versus MCC and UEE versus Clarke, but feelings between individual players don't seem to have been so acute as might be thought. In successive matches during August, the supposed antagonists played together in three successive matches. During the Canterbury Festival, Kent played England: since, however, a normal eleven-a-side contest would have been very unequal, Kent now being very weak, William Clarke, John Wisden, John Bickley and George Parr were all co-opted into the Kent eleven, with Wisden and Clarke opening the Kent attack, whilst James Dean and Jemmy Grundy opened the bowling for England. England won by seven wickets and Fred Lillywhite commented: 'The opinion generally expressed was that the selection of the four players (for Kent) was not good, considering they had the scope of England.' This on the face of it seems a rather biased remark.

Many of the players involved in the Canterbury match moved directly on to Brighton where Sussex, with William Clarke and George Parr, as given men, opposed an England eleven. Lillywhite comments: 'The match originated from someone whose judgment was not altogether sound.' However, Lillywhite then rather negates his derogatory remark with the following notes: 'The selection of those "given" Wisden and Clarke again joined together as opening bowlers and shared all 20 England wickets between them, as Sussex won by 68 runs; Dean in the Sussex team hit the highest score in the match.'

Having completed the Sussex match, the group of players proceeded to Nottingham for the start of play on Monday of Nottinghamshire v England. Unlike Kent and Sussex, Notts did not demand any 'given' men. The England side was chosen by MCC, rather than by Clarke, so Wisden and Dean were among the visitors to Trent Bridge. England won in two days by an innings. The report in the *Nottingham Review* attributes the county's defeat in part to poor fielding. Lillywhite states Notts had difficulty raising their strongest side (Bickley and Frank Tinley were absent). Clarke bowled most overs for Notts but was no more expensive than his colleagues, and the cry that he did not know when to take himself off couldn't be justly levelled against him on this occasion. From Trent Bridge, the Notts team went straight down to Surrey, not to The Oval, due to a dispute with the lessee, but to Broadwater Park, the home of the Marshall family. The pitch was dreadful: Julius Caesar, playing for Surrey, decided the only tactic in the circumstances was to hit out. Lillywhite notes: 'he not only went effectually to the slows, but "jumped off" at Bickley and Grundy, and punished them in that manner somewhat severely.' Caesar, hitting the highest two scores in the match, won the game for his side.

The season ended with an almost continuous programme of All-England matches – from 28 August to 27 September, the team had just one three-day break and won six out of eight games. Lillywhite credits Clarke with twice as many wickets as any other bowler; Clarke took 476 wickets, Wisden 210 and Dean 191. The All-England Eleven engaged two new recruits during the season, H.H.Stephenson (Surrey) and Edgar Willsher (Kent), both appearing in 15 of the 24 matches. The two old stagers who reduced their appearances markedly were Alfred Mynn and William Hillyer; Mynn was now 47 and Hillyer 41. Stephenson was 21 and Willsher 25 – both had distinguished careers ahead of them and both played for the AEE during Clarke's final seasons and continued under Parr's leadership.

Chapter Ten
The Last Summers

The three or four known extant letters written, or perhaps dictated, by Clarke all date from the winter of 1855/56 and are simply routine correspondence regarding confirmation of AEE fixtures. They are all written on printed notepaper headed 'Anglesea Hotel, W.' The letter Clarke wrote to *The Era* newspaper in December 1852 gives Clarke's address as 'Anglesea Hotel, Haymarket'. The hotel was situated at No.64 on the west side of the road; the site is now occupied by a cinema (built in 1927 as the Carlton Theatre). It would seem most likely that Clarke used the Anglesea as his headquarters during the close season, at least from 1852/53 to 1855/56. The hotel dates from about 1842 and was still being used in 1860. Newspaper references to it indicate that it was a place frequented by sporting gentlemen mainly, but not entirely connected with the turf and the hotelkeeper from 1845 was Edmund Wright (mis-spelt as Waight in the printed version of the 1851 census).

In various reminiscences Clarke is mentioned as a shrewd betting man, and this venue would seem to confirm that. If the two assumptions – that Clarke lived in relative winter comfort in an Haymarket hotel and that he was partial to putting money on horses – are taken as fact, they support the suggestion (in the absence of any will) that Clarke died leaving little in the way of cash. In short it appears that he readily spent all he earned.

The summer of 1855 saw Clarke, now 56, begin his fortieth season of major cricket, according to Fred Lillywhite 'a longer career than any other cricketer of note'. Nottinghamshire had played four matches in 1854, two each against England and against Surrey. There were no *bona fide* Nottinghamshire matches in 1855 – though one had been arranged and advertised, against Surrey at The Oval, but did not materialize. One assumes petty squabbling was the cause, but the Nottingham papers don't appear to give any cogent reason.

Clarke arranged 24 All-England matches, roughly the same number as in the three preceding summers. For the first time since the initial season, these fixtures did not begin until June. Was old age catching up with him?

Clarke's first match of the summer was for North v South at Lord's on 28 and 29 May. The Northern eleven was chosen by his friend the Hon Frederick Ponsonby. Whether Ponsonby over-ruled his fellow members of the MCC Committee, or whether the Committee decided to rescind the ban they had imposed on Clarke is not known, but Clarke played a major role in the match. Fred Lillywhite notes: 'The Hon Frederick Ponsonby used his best and able judgment in selecting the North side, while the South "team" was brought together by that influential and liberal supporter of cricket, the Hon R.Grimston.'

The North scored 103; the South replied with 144. The North's second innings amounted to 111, leaving the South a mere 71 runs for victory, half their first innings total. Clarke and Bickley opened the North's bowling and dismissed their opponents for 52! Clarke, now aged 56, sent down 18 overs for 25 runs and took six wickets. He bowled unchanged with Bickley. As Lillywhite notes: 'A great deal of money changed hands.'

Clarke went to The Oval for the next match – Surrey v England. The match had been arranged by Clarke, and therefore all the United England players declined to appear. The Surrey County Cricket Club had this season taken control of The Oval, William Houghton (the lessee) having decided to leave, so this was the first important fixture under the new arrangement. Clarke and Bickley again bowled unchanged to dismiss Surrey in their first innings for 67 – Clarke four for 43, Bickley five for 24. With George Parr hitting 50, the England team obtained a good lead, being 148 all out. Despite Clarke taking a further five wickets in Surrey's second innings, England required 87 for victory, but won by only one wicket. Clarke was undefeated with a single run to his name, though smarter fielding by Surrey should have run out Clarke's partner, Brown, as the winning run was made.

Clarke's cricket continued with nine All-England matches, including a game at Reading when he took 20 wickets, and the match at Trent Bridge with Nottingham Commercial, Clarke taking 19 wickets for 79 runs. The *Nottingham Review* commented: 'The slow, dodging peculiars of our old favourite cricketer and townsman, Bill Clark, proved most effective.'

On July 12 Clarke was unable to play for the AEE v Melton Mowbray due to 'bad eyes' and missed that game and the six AEE fixtures which followed. One of these was at Bristol against XXII of West Gloucestershire. Clarke, according to W.G.Grace's biography *Cricket*, had written to Grace's father stating that he would not be able to play due to 'ill-health and failing eyesight'. Clarke did, however, attend the match and was so impressed by the fielding (at long stop) of 13-year-old E.M.Grace, that he presented E.M., W.G.'s older brother, with a bat and, at the end of the match, gave Mrs Grace a copy of Bolland's book. Clarke had met the Grace family during the corresponding fixture in 1854 and W.G. claims that this latter game was his first memory of watching a major cricket match.

The single match involving Nottinghamshire in 1855 was a rather odd contest at Trent Bridge in the middle of August with the opponents described as Five of Kent and Six of England. Lillywhite comments: 'One might imagine that England was not sufficiently strong to play Nottingham, without the assistance of Kent, or vice-versa.' Haygarth points out that none of the United Eleven played, except Grundy, because the match was arranged by Clarke, but Lillywhite seems more attuned to the events, pointing out that neither the North Kent group nor those at Canterbury approved of the match and therefore Kent couldn't field a representative eleven and had, in effect, six given men. The visitors won by seven wickets.

The *Nottingham Review,* rather in contrast to the paper's early note, stated: Although much as we admire the abilities and perseverance of our old townsman W.Clark, we cannot refrain from saying that it is our opinion, and also the opinion of his best friends, that the match would have looked much better had he taken himself off bowling, for, from the nature of the ground (which is truth itself) and the splendid play of Adams and Anderson, it was impossible for him to be successful. Indeed it is a fault of his not to know the exact time when to cease bowling.'

The *Review*'s remark came after the first innings, when Clarke bowled unchanged for 68 overs, taking six wickets for 92, including those of Anderson and Caesar. It was to prove Clarke's final match for his county. (It was also the last match in which Clarke participated that the ACS has ranked as first-class.) From the close of the 1854 season the committee of the County Cricket Club seems to have become dormant once more. Clarke organized this 1855 game. In 1856 the only county fixture was against England at Newark and no matches at all were played in 1857.

Whether or not Clarke read the comment in the *Nottingham Review,* the number of overs he bowled in the remaining seven AEE matches of 1855 was quite formidable. Between 20 August and 19 September, Clarke bowled in 14 innings. The figures, four-ball overs of course, are set out below:

Dates	Opponents	First	Second	Total
20, 21 and 22 August	Dudley	22	48*	70
23, 24 and 25 August	Leicestershire	40	78*	118
27, 28 and 29 August	Hereford	39.2	17*	56.2
3, 4 and 5 September	Nottingham Commercial	39*	43.2	82.2*
6, 7 and 8 September	Leeds	41*	29.1	70.1
10, 11 and 12 September	Cheshire	28*	49*	77*
17, 18 and 19 September	Hull	38*	46*	84*

Total 558.1

Note: Asterisks denote Clarke bowling unchanged through the innings or match concerned. The opposition were twenty-twos apart from Nottingham Commercial who comprised eighteen.

The fact that Clarke bowled unchanged through what would prove (with a minor exception in 1856) the final four innings of his long career is uncanny, almost as if he knew the end had come. To add to the surreal aspect of those matches, the side, which Clarke had single-handedly created, was undefeated, winning four and drawing the others. The AEE match against Nottingham Commercial was staged on The Forest ground, the original venue for so many of Clarke's early matches, but not one on which he had played for many years. The game was arranged as a benefit for the Notts wicketkeeper, Charley Brown, and it is stated in the press that 10,000 attended each day – admission of course was free – almost as if the Nottingham public foresaw that this would be Clarke's last appearance in a cricket match in the county of his birth. Fred Lillywhite notes that Charley Brown had a disagreement with the gentlemen who ran county cricket at Trent Bridge, hence the venue. Clarke took 277 wickets for the All-England Eleven in this his last complete season.

The programme for All-England matches for 1856 comprised 21 matches, beginning at Christ Church, Oxford, the most aristocratic of the Oxford colleges, on 15 May. Clarke was not in the eleven, but appeared in the next two fixtures at Durham on 19 to 21 May and at Neath on 2 to 4 June, though only as a batsman. The AEE then went on to Cirencester and Downham Market before going up to Whitehaven in Cumberland. Missing those first two games, Clarke appeared in the last of these fixtures and put himself on to bowl in the closing minutes of Whitehaven's first innings, taking two wickets for 13 in 9.1 overs. He captured the final wicket – J.Towerson, possibly one of two Johns resident in the town according to the 1851 Census – who was stumped by George Morton for none. Haygarth states Clarke was 'very weak'.

Three more AEE fixtures were completed before the team arrived at Melton Mowbray for the match played on 10, 11 and 12 July. William Clarke officiated as an umpire. Fred Lillywhite notes: 'it was the last match in which the renowned slow bowler, Clarke, took any part.' It is worthy of note that the ground at Melton is still known as the All England Cricket Ground – the venue off Saxby Road currently contains both rugby and cricket pitches. The details of very few Trent Bridge matches are published in the Nottingham newspapers in 1856 and the few that do appear feature Nottingham Amateurs CC – the only Nottinghamshire game was played at Newark in August, as previously noted.

In order to obtain some relief from his ailments, Clarke travelled from Melton to the then spa town of Askern, about four miles north of Doncaster and known for its medical waters. He stayed for four weeks, but did not recover and moved to London, to Priory Lodge, Wandsworth Road, Kennington, some 15 minutes' walk from The Oval. (The area these days is in the Battersea postal district.) In an 1849 trade directory a building known as the 'Priory' at the corner of Priory Road and Wandsworth Road (South) was listed as a Ladies School – it is shown as a large house about three times the size of surrounding properties. In an 1853 directory 'Priory Lodge' is occupied by Henry Wilson on the north side of Wandsworth Road on the estate of Springfield House. This area was extensively redeveloped during the latter half of the nineteenth century with the construction of Nine Elms railway depot. Much of this is now the New Covent Garden fruit and vegetable market. It was at Priory Lodge that William Clarke died on 25 August 1856, cause of death 'paraplegia'; witness at death Henry W. Petty. According to the *Nottinghamshire Guardian*, he had been 'long suffering under a severe and protracted attack of paralysis'. Paralysis of the lower half of the body is often caused by a spinal-cord injury.

The All-England Eleven began a match at Loughborough against a local Twenty-Two on 25 August. On learning of his father's imminent demise, Alfred Clarke left the game, but arrived in London too late to see his father alive. He was buried in the South Metropolitan Cemetery, West Norwood on 30 August, when the Eleven were fulfilling a fixture at Hull. William Clarke died intestate and there seems to be no way of discovering the value of his estate, but since no stone was erected to mark his burial place it would appear likely that William Clarke left little money and that his son, Alfred, was not a person of means in 1856. When I went in search of Clarke's grave in the 1960s, I found a wilderness of weeds and brambles but no headstone. Some ten years ago this lack of any positive marking of Clarke's last resting place in the cemetery was remedied by Alex Picker, a young enthusiast employed at the time by Nottinghamshire County Cricket Club, and due solely to his efforts money was raised to produce and erect a suitable memorial there.

Seek and ye shall find. The author failing to identify William Clarke's unmarked grave at West Norwood in 1969.

Chapter Eleven

Postscript

Clarke's second wife, Mary, had moved from the Trent Bridge Inn to the home of her son, John Chapman, by the time of the 1851 census, as noted earlier. In 1861 she moved to the South Nottinghamshire village of Rempstone, where she took a house and at least in the 1861 and 1871 censuses lived alone, being shown as an 'annuitant'. In 1881 she is living with the Jacobs family in Main Street, Rempstone as a boarder, but described as an 'independent lady', aged 93. She died in Rempstone and was buried in Rempstone All Saints churchyard on 7 December 1885, aged 97, under the name Mary Chapman, though her death was registered as Mary Clark. For someone of such a great age, one might expect an obituary in the local papers, but none seem to have been published.

Her son, John Chapman, remained in Gainsborough for the rest of his life. When he had moved to the town he had five children aged 10, 7, 6, 4 and 2. Three more were added, making in all six sons and two daughters. His wife, Jane (née Richards) died in 1873 and twenty years later he was married a second time, to Mary Ann Thompson, 48 years his junior. He took an active part in the cricket of Gainsborough for many years; he continued his veterinary practice through the rest of his life, being in his 80s one of the oldest members of the Royal College of Veterinary Surgeons.

He died suddenly at home on 14 April 1896 soon after having eaten his dinner. This unexpected death brought about a coroner's inquiry. The chief witness was his young wife; the press report states that her evidence was 'very loose throughout'. There was a suspicion of poison, either self-administered or given by another. His wife stated that her husband unlocked a dresser drawer and took out a bottle with a red label. He could have either drunk from the bottle, or added the contents to a cup of whiskey which she brought him. She threw the bottle in the fire and poured the rest of the contents of the cup on the floor. The doctor was called after Chapman collapsed, but was unable to revive him. However, the doctor stated he could find no evidence of poison and the verdict was returned of death from apoplexy or natural causes. Mrs Chapman stated that his insurance had lapsed.

The *Gainsborough News* published a long obituary, which detailed his cricket career at Trent Bridge and mentioned him playing with such cricketers as Alfred Mynn and Fuller Pilch, adding, 'His father and he practically made the famous Trent Bridge Ground.' Nowhere in the notice is there a mention of William Clarke. The piece contains a charming description of Chapman himself:

Many of us will take long to forget the hale and hearty old man with his rubicund visage, white whiskers and long hat, and nothing the matter with him but 'this blessed sciatica, you know, Mr William, God bless the Queen.' He was nothing if not loyal. Up early in the morning he enjoyed and appreciated nature at its best and he delighted in his profession.

Clarke himself had seven children by his first wife, Jane (née Wigley). Frances, baptised at St Nicholas, Nottingham on 3 August 1820, died aged seven and was buried at St Nicholas on 9 December 1827. The two next boys in the family, John, baptised at St Nicholas on 18 August 1823, and William, baptised at St Nicholas on 21 September 1826, both joined the Army and were drafted to India. William appears in three published cricket matches in India in 1847, 1848 and 1851. John Clarke of the 10th (Lincolnshire) Regiment of Foot died on a date unknown – his name is on the memorial in Lincoln Cathedral. William Clarke of the 32nd Regiment of Foot died of wounds on 2 August 1857. The eldest, Mary, born in 1818 has not been traced.

William Clarke's third daughter, Matilda, was baptised at St Nicholas on 1 September 1824 and married George Gunn of Normanton-on-the-Wolds at Old Radford Church, Nottingham; Gunn worked at the Flying Horse, Poultry, Nottingham. It would appear there were no children of the marriage. William Clarke's fourth daughter, Jane, was baptised on 19 October 1828 and married twice, first John Hardy (1831-1859) and second, James Borrington. She is the only one of William Clarke's children included in the 1841 census for the Trent Bridge Inn. She died on 25 October 1908 in Derby.

William Clarke's fourth daughter, Jane, outlived two husbands; this photograph dates from about 1900, when she was 72.

Finally William Clarke's youngest child, Alfred, was born at the Bell Inn, Angel Row and baptised at St Nicholas on 21 February 1830. Probably because of William Clarke's abrupt departure from Nottingham when Alfred was 16, there seem to be no references in the Nottingham newspapers to Alfred playing cricket in local matches – I presume he played outside the county. His debut for the All-England Eleven occurred on 19 June 1851 and is explained by Fred Lillywhite's notes in the 1852 edition of the *Guide*: 'Clark, A. of Nottingham, son of the veteran, is the scorer for the [All-England] Eleven and played two matches for them; he is a very excellent field.' He played in eight AEE matches the following summer; thereafter he was a permanent member of the All-England team. How long previous to 1851 he had acted as the team's scorer is not known, but possibly at the same time he also took on the role of sorting out the travel arrangements as other commentators refer to him as being known as the team's 'Bradshaw'. His debut for Nottinghamshire was also in 1851, when he was a last minute replacement for R.C.Tinley.

Alfred married Eliza Oliver in 1859 and they had two children, William Oliver, who died aged 15 in 1875 and Sarah Jane, born 1863, who married Alfred Wilson and had four children, Florence (b 1884), Alfred (b 1886), Eliza (b 1888) and Daisy (b 1890). Alfred Clarke's county career ran parallel to his matches for AEE. He went to Australia with Parr's side in 1863/64; his final county game was in 1863 and final AEE match the next summer. His last appearance in *Lillywhite's Guides* occurs in the 1865 edition: 'Clarke, Alfred, born at Nottingham February 16, 1831 [sic] was only to be seen in those matches against Twenty-twos, consequently not under much notice. He has been a fast-improving cricketer since his first appearance in the field, but has now taken to business.' From 1856 he was also the cricket coach at Rossall School until the early 1860s. Alfred Clarke died at his home in Ruddington, just outside Nottingham on 23 October 1878. He is buried in Ruddington churchyard where a stone to his memory still stands – the stone also gives the details of his son, William Oliver.

With William Clarke's death, the management and captaincy of the All-England Eleven was taken over by George Parr, and in 1858 *Lillywhite's Guide* lists the members of the All-England Eleven committee as Julius Caesar, Edgar Willsher, H.H.Stephenson, Alfred Clarke and George Anderson. On 1 June 1857 at Lord's, the All-England Eleven met the United for the first time before what was described as the largest crowd seen on the ground for a long time. *Lillywhite* comments:

> The amalgamation of both Elevens, who strove to serve each other, was universally admired. It is hoped such cordiality and good feeling will continue to exist between these two celebrated bodies, and that each will boldly contest against all personal allusions coming from persons who are not sufficiently acquainted with the 'manners and customs' to form any judgment upon the matter.

The two rival teams continued to play against each other until 1869, when the United was disbanded – in November 1864 a large group of the United players had announced that they would no longer play for that team, still under the management of John Wisden, and formed a new professional body, the United South of England Eleven. This schism seriously weakened the United Eleven and it limped on for several seasons before its demise. Clarke's AEE continued, but fixtures grew fewer and probably the arrival of the Australians in 1878 saw its virtual closure. The USEE, with W.G.Grace as its star attraction, continued on a low-key basis for some further years.

Nottinghamshire, insofar as inter-county cricket was concerned, was a shadow of what it ought to have been, given the quality of players available to make up an eleven in the mid-1850s. Surprisingly there were no inter-county matches at Trent Bridge from 1855, when there was a single match against England, Clarke captaining the county until 1860, when Surrey were the visitors. John Johnson, the Nottingham solicitor, effectively took control and one can say a new era began with the first Notts Colts trial at Easter in 1861.

When William Clarke assumed control of the Nottingham Old Club in 1830, he had simply continued the *modus operandi* by which the top level of Nottingham cricket had been run since the 1770s. After he died George Parr followed in his footsteps, but through the 1860s worked in collaboration with the County Cricket Committee created by John Johnson. Once Parr retired, the Committee, elected annually by subscribers to the County Cricket Club, took over the running and financing of representative county teams. Yorkshire county cricket evolved via Sheffield in a similar manner, but almost all the other county sides developed, not through professional players organizing themselves, but through the landed gentry of the county.

Alex Picker with William Clarke's gravestone in West Norwood Cemetery.

Acknowledgements

There can be very few people who have innocently drifted into the library at Trent Bridge Cricket Ground in the last two years and not been inflicted by my William Clarke 'problem'. In other words at the time of their arrival whatever piece of the Clarke jigsaw I was trying to find.

Those who are regular library users suffered even greater pain. I thank you all for putting up with my tales of woe and sometimes suggesting books that might provide the solution and at other times going home to play with their computers to see if the answer was hidden somewhere in the ether. Keith Warsop and Martin Wilson read through the first draft and kindly made corrections and suggestions. David Jeater acted as the final editor on behalf of the publishers; he suggested a number of additional paragraphs by way of explanation. These have largely been incorporated and will assist the general reader to understand more readily the circumstances of the age in which Clarke flourished.

I have tried to recall all the brave souls who helped; if I've inadvertently omitted your name from the following, please forgive me: Duncan Anderson, David Beaumont, Steve Bilton, Rob Brooke, Derek Drake, Angela Geddes, John and Michael Goulder, David Gretton, Duncan Hamilton, Jerry Lodge, Chris O'Brien, Mick Pope, Malcolm Powell, Claire Webberley, Steve Zaleski. Derek Drake also contributed to much of the statistical material.

In the production of the book itself I wish to thank City Press Leeds for their attention to the detail of typesetting; to Roger Mann and Richard Shaw for their help with illustrations; to David Taylor for his indexing; and to Kit Bartlett and Jenny Moulton for their proofreading.

P.W-T.
West Bridgford, Nottinghamshire
June 2014

Bibliography

Newspapers

The files of the leading Nottingham newspapers have been extensively searched, particularly the *Nottingham Journal* and the *Nottingham Review*. Other local newspapers have been checked especially for reports of specific All-England Eleven matches during the period up to Clarke's death. The *Gainsborough News* provided information on the death and subsequent inquest regarding John Chapman.

Books

Amey, Geoff., *Julius Caesar: The Ill-Fated Cricketer*, Bodyline Books, 2000

Ashley-Cooper, F.S., *Nottinghamshire Cricket and Cricketers*, Saxton, 1923

Bailey, Philip (ed), *[Important] Cricket Matches, 1826 to 1856*, ACS, various years

Bolland, William, *Cricket Notes*, Trelawney, Saunders, 1851

Box, Charles, *The English Game of Cricket*, The Field, 1877

Brodribb, Gerald, *Felix on the Bat*, Eyre and Spottiswoode, 1962

Brodribb, Gerald, *Felix and the England Eleven*, Boundary Books Ltd, 2002

Browne, Edwin, *Nottinghamshire Cricket*, Geo Richards, 1887

Caffyn, William, *Seventy-One Not Out*, William Blackwood and Sons, 1899

Courtney, S, *As Centuries Blend (Clydesdale C.C.)*, John Miller Ltd, 1954

Daft, Richard, *Kings of Cricket*, Arrowsmith, 1893

Felix, Nicholas, *How to Play Clarke*, Baily Bros, 1852

Grace, W.G., *Cricket*, Arrowsmith, 1891

Haygarth, A., *Scores and Biographies, Vols 1 to 5*, Lillywhite/MCC, various years

Harris, Lord and Ashley-Cooper, F.S., *Lord's and the M.C.C.*,
    London and Counties Press Association, 1914

Jenkinson, Neil, *Richard Daft: On a Pedestal, ACS Publications, 2008*

Lillywhite, Frederick, *The Guide to Cricketers*, Lillywhite, various years

Mitchell, B.R., *British Historical Statistics*, Cambridge University Press, 1988

Montcrieff, W., *Reminiscences of Grange Cricket Club*, David Douglas, 1891

Morrah, Patrick, *Alfred Mynn and the Cricketers of his Time*,
    Eyre and Spottiswoode, 1963

Pullin, A.W., *Talks with Old English Cricketers*, William Blackwood and Sons, 1900

Pycroft, James, *The Cricket Field*, Longman, Green, Longman, 1851

Rendell, Brian, *Fuller Pilch: A Straightforward Man*, ACS Publications, 2010

Rait Kerr, R.S., *The Laws of Cricket: Their History and Growth*,
    Longmans, Green and Co, 1950

Richards, C.H., *Fifty Years of Nottinghamshire Cricket*, Geo Richards, 1890

Sissons, Ric, 'William Clarke' in *Oxford Dictionary of National Biography, Vol 11*,
    pp 926-927, Oxford University Press, 2004

Sutton, A.K., *Nottinghamshire Cricket Matches: 1771-1865*, Sutton, 1865

Vamplew, Wray, *Play Up and Play the Game*, Cambridge University Press, 1988

West, G.Derek, *The Elevens of England*, Darf, 1988

Guide to Important Cricket Matches Played in the British Isles: 1707-1863, ACS, 1981

Appendix One

Career Statistics

First-class Cricket

The statistical details given below relate to Clarke's performances in matches identified as first-class by the Association of Cricket Statisticians and Historians and listed in its 1996 publication *Complete First-Class Match List: Volume I, 1801-1914*. The figures take into account match details found by researchers in recent years.

First-class cricket: Batting and Fielding

Season	M	I	NO	Runs	HS	Ave	50	Ct
1826	1	2	0	13	8	6.50	0	0
1827	2	3	0	31	17	10.33	0	2
1828	3	6	0	67	31	11.16	0	3
1829	2	4	0	53	41	13.25	0	0
1830	1	2	0	70	59	35.00	1	1
1831	1	2	0	35	18	17.50	0	0
1832	1	2	0	25	25	12.50	0	1
1834	3	4	0	102	65	25.50	1	0
1835	2	3	0	10	6	3.33	0	0
1836	1	1	0	4	4	4.00	0	1
1837	1	2	0	20	13	10.00	0	2
1840	4	7	0	142	57	20.28	1	4
1841	2	4	0	21	18	5.25	0	1
1842	2	4	0	131	75	32.75	1	2
1843	5	8	0	111	30	13.87	0	1
1844	4	7	0	68	25	9.71	0	2
1845	6	10	0	66	21	6.60	0	4
1846	9	17	3	155	65	11.07	1	4
1847	13	25	2	308	50	13.39	1	4
1848	9	16	0	112	22	7.00	0	3
1849	14	23	2	200	71	9.52	1	5
1850	10	16	1	143	28	9.53	0	0
1851	14	22	9	81	22*	6.23	0	6
1852	11	13	5	49	14	6.12	0	1
1853	12	20	8	73	10*	6.08	0	5
1854	7	14	5	36	15	4.00	0	2
1855	3	6	2	7	4	1.75	0	1
Totals	**143**	**243**	**37**	**2133**	**75**	**10.35**	**7**	**55**

Notes: Clarke was dismissed 86 times bowled (42%); 76 times caught (37%); 23 times run out (11%); 12 times stumped (6%) and nine times lbw (4%); he was never dismissed hit wicket.

First-class cricket: Bowling

Season	O	M	R	W	Ave	BB	5wi	10wi
1826	76.3	13	161	5	32.20	5/161	1	-
1827	?	?	?	0 + [8]	?	5/?	1	-
1828	?	?	?	0 + [12]	?	5/?	1	-
1830	?	?	?	0 + [1]	?	1/?	-	-
1831	?	?	?	0 + [5]	?	4/?	-	-
1832	?	?	?	0 + [1]	?	1/?	-	-
1837	27	?	38	4	9.50	3/15	-	-
1840	?	?	?	0 + [24]	?	9/?	2	1
1841	32	9	51	5 + [1]	10.20	5/51	1	-
1842	75	28	108	7 + [4]	15.42	7/98	1	-
1843	122.1	42	75	20 + [30]	3.75	7/17	5	3
1844	197.1	30	262	32	8.18	6/26	3	1
1845	319.1	38	327	36 + [28]	9.08	9/29	8	4
1846	51	9	108	11 + [28]	9.81	6/?	3	1
1847	110	?	162	15 + [45]	10.80	7/?	5	1
1848	130	23	87	5 + [42]	17.40	7/?	4	1
1849	248.3	104	242	38 + [36]	6.36	7/11	9	3
1850	166.3	45	199	31 + [43]	6.41	9/34	10	3
1851	290	74	328	34 + [50]	9.64	8/35	8	2
1852	543.2	212	804	69	11.65	9/80	8	3
1853	571.1	274	631	49	12.87	6/37	4	-
1854	456.2	164	645	51	12.64	8/47	5	2
1855	198.1	40	303	27	11.22	6/25	4	1
Totals	**3615.2**	**1105**	**4531**	**439 + [358]**	**10.32**	**9/29**	**83**	**26**

Notes: Clarke did not bowl in first-class matches in 1829, 1834, 1835 and 1836. Overs were of four balls throughout his career. Full analyses are not available for all Clarke's matches; in the wickets column the figures in brackets relate to matches where runs conceded figures are not known. The averages given in these years relate only to matches where runs conceded figures are known. Of his 797 wickets, 359 (45%) were bowled; 311 (39%) were caught; 99 (12%, a high proportion) were stumped; 15 (2%) were hit wicket and 13 (2%) were lbw. In matches where full figures are available he took wickets at a rate of one per 29.80 balls, and conceded runs at a rate equivalent to 2.07 per six-ball over.

First-Class Cricket: Fifties (7)

Score	For	Opponent	Venue	Season
59	Nottingham	Sheffield	Sheffield	1830
65	Nottingham	Sheffield	Sheffield	1834
57	North	MCC	Burton upon Trent	1840
75	Players of Notts	Gentlemen of Notts	Trent Bridge	1842
65	MCC	Sussex	Brighton	1846
50	MCC	Sussex	Lord's	1847
71	Married	Single	Lord's	1849

Note: All Clarke's fifties were in the first innings.

First-Class Cricket: Seven or more wickets in an innings (25)

Analysis	For	Opponent	Venue	Season
?-?-?-9	Nottinghamshire	Kent[2]	Town Malling	1840
68-25-98-7	Nottinghamshire	England[1]	Trent Bridge	1842
32.1-?-?-7	Nottinghamshire	MCC[2]	Lord's	1843
28-14-28-7	Nottinghamshire	MCC[2]	Trent Bridge	1843
18.2-14-17-7	Nottinghamshire	Sussex[1]	Trent Bridge	1843
?-?-?-7	North	MCC[1]	Lord's	1844
27-11-29-9	Nottinghamshire	Kent[1]	Trent Bridge	1845
29-8-40-7	Nottinghamshire	Kent[2]	Trent Bridge	1845
40-?-?-7	England	Kent[2]	Canterbury	1845
50-14-89-7	North	MCC[1]	Trent Bridge	1845
?-?-?-7	Suffolk	MCC[2]	Lord's	1848
?-?-?-7	North	MCC[1]	Lord's	1848
29-18-29-7	All-England Eleven	Hampshire[1]	Southampton	1849
34.3-15-46-7	All-England Eleven	Hampshire[2]	Southampton	1849
?-?-?-7	England	Surrey[2]	The Oval	1849
24.2-16-11-7	North	South[1]	Leamington Spa	1849
20-?-34-9	All-England Eleven	Yorkshire[1]	Sheffield	1850
?-?-?-7	Players	Gentlemen[2]	Lord's	1850
28-11-35-8	All-England Eleven	MCC and Metropolitan Clubs	Lord's	1851
?-?-?-7	All-England Eleven	MCC[2]	Lord's	1851
49-?-51-7	North	South[1]	The Oval	1851
30-11-47-8	North	South[2]	The Oval	1851
40-9-80-8	All-England Eleven	Yorkshire[1]	Sheffield	1852
44-16-80-9	All-England Eleven	Yorkshire[2]	Sheffield	1852
36-17-47-8	Nottinghamshire	Surrey[2]	Trent Bridge	1854

Note: The index figures [1] and [2] above indicate the innings in which the feat was achieved.

Principal Matches

The details below relate to the important matches played by Clarke starting from his debut for the Nottingham Old Club in 1816, aged 17. He will have played in other matches for which researchers may yet discover details, or which went unrecorded.

Principal Matches: Batting and Fielding

Season	M	I	NO	Runs	HS	Ave	Ct
1816	1	1	0	0	0	0.00	0
1817	2	3	0	4	3	1.33	0
1818	1	1	0	6	6	6.00	3
1821	2	3	0	32	18	10.66	0
1822	3	4	0	61	45	15.25	2
1823	2	3	0	28	23	9.33	6
1825	1	2	0	15	13	7.50	0
1826	1	2	0	13	8	6.50	0
1827	2	3	0	31	17	10.33	2
1828	3	6	0	67	31	11.16	3
1829	4	8	1	107	41	15.28	1
1830	1	2	0	70	59	35.00	1

1831	1	2	0	35	18	17.50	0
1832	1	2	0	25	25	12.50	1
1833	1	2	0	2	1	1.00	0
1834	3	4	0	102	65	25.50	0
1835	2	3	0	10	6	3.33	0
1836	1	1	0	4	4	4.00	0
1837	1	2	0	20	13	10.00	2
1840	3	5	0	77	22	15.40	4
1841	1	2	0	1	1	0.50	1
1842	2	4	0	131	75	32.75	2
1843	5	8	0	111	30	13.87	1
1844	2	4	0	53	25	13.25	2
1845	6	10	0	66	21	6.60	3
1846	12	22	4	175	65	9.72	7
1847	23	42	4	434	50	11.42	6
1848	22	38	2	254	34	7.05	11
1849	31	52	6	345	71	7.50	11
1850	31	51	7	320	28	7.25	4
1851	36	57	17	276	72	6.90	12
1852	33	46	18	117	14	4.17	11
1853	34	53	15	184	15	4.84	16
1854	30	51	18	157	17	4.75	11
1855	20	32	0	75	12	2.34	11
1856	3	5	0	3	3	0.60	0
Total	**327**	**536**	**101**	**3402**	**75**	**7.82**	**134**

Principal Matches: Bowling

Season	O	M	Runs	W	Ave	TW
1816-1825				[27]		27
1826	76.3	13	161	5	32.20	5
1827				[8]	8	
1828				[10]	10	
1829				[1]	1	
1830				[1]	1	
1831				[5]	5	
1832				[1]	1	
1833				[3]	3	
1834				[0]	0	
1835				[0]	0	
1836				[0]	0	
1837	27	?	38	4	9.50	4
1840				[22]	22	
1841	32	9	51	5 + [1]	10.20	6
1842	75	28	108	7 + [4]	15.42	11
1843	72.2	42	75	20 + [30]	3.75	50
1844	116.2	30	152	14 +	10.85	14
1845	134	19	170	23 + [41]	7.39	64
1846	48	(8)	101	12 + [28]	8.41	40
1847	99	?	187	18 + [88]	10.38	106
1848	317.2	128	364	68 + [120]	5.35	188
1849	807	382	961	163 + [108]	5.89	271
1850	449	142	552	92 + [233]	6.00	325

1851	1455.1	648	1615	294 + [50]	5.49	344
1852	1950.2	855	2141	390 + [44]	5.48	434
1853	1721.3	886	1778	301 + [67]	5.90	368
1854	626.2	246	896	80 + [397]	11.20	477
1855	1433.2	(42)	1852	295	6.27	295
1856	9.1	?	13	2	7.50	2
Total	**9451**	**11215**	**1793**	**+ [1289]**	**6.25**	**3082**

Notes: Overs were of four balls throughout his career. Full analyses are not available for all Clarke's matches; in the wickets column the figures in brackets relate to matches where runs conceded figures are not known. The averages given in these years relate only to matches where runs conceded figures are known. Figures in the column headed TW give the total number of wickets he took in principal matches.

All-England Eleven matches

The details below relate to all the matches played by Clarke for the All-England Eleven, both eleven-a-side and against odds, which he managed for eleven seasons. The figures are derived mainly from match scores in Haygarth's *Scores and Biographies*, but with amendments derived from more recent researches.

All-England Eleven: Batting and Fielding

Season	M	I	NO	Runs	HS	Ave	Ct
1846	3	5	1	20	14	5.00	3
1847	10	17	2	126	22	8.40	2
1848	15	26	2	180	34	7.50	9
1849	20	33	6	183	19	6.77	7
1850	24	41	6	223	28	6.37	4
1851	27	44	11	219	72	6.63	7
1852	24	34	13	75	9*	3.57	10
1853	23	34	7	121	15	4.48	11
1854	23	37	13	121	17	5.04	9
1855	18	28	8	70	12	3.50	11
1856	3	5	0	3	3	0.60	0
Totals	**190**	**304**	**69**	**1341**	**72**	**5.70**	**73**

All-England Eleven: Bowling

Season	O	M	Runs	W	Ave	TW
1846	8	?	21	1	21.00	1
1847	10	?	25	3 + [43]	8.33	46
1848	317.1	128	364	68 + [78]	5.35	146
1849	749.2	343	914	151 + [74]	6.05	225
1850	392	118	480	84+ [188]	5.71	272
1851	1335.1	627	1451	274 + [12]	5.29	286
1852	1549.1	702	1537	343 + [44]	4.48	387
1853	1256	679	1240	257 + [67]	4.82	324
1854	170	82	251	29 + [397]	8.65	426
1855	1311.2	31	1643	277	5.93	277
1856	9.1	?	13	2	6.50	2
Total	**7108**	**2710**	**7939**	**1489 + [903]**	**5.33**	**2392**

Notes: As with similar tables above, overs were of four balls throughout Clarke's career. In the wickets column the figures in brackets relate to matches where runs conceded figures are not known. The averages given in these years relate only to matches where runs conceded figures are known. Figures in the column headed TW give the total number of wickets he took in All-England matches.

Sources: Haygarth, A., *Scores and Biographies, Vols 1 to 5,* Lillywhite/MCC, various years; and various contemporary newspapers.

Appendix Two
Practical Hints on Cricket

Set out below is a full version of our subject's advice to cricketers, which originally appeared in William Bolland's *Cricket Notes* published in 1851, over the name of William Clark [sic], slow bowler and secretary to the All-England Eleven, and dedicated to Hon Frederick Ponsonby.

I
The Science of Bowling

The merit of Bowling in my opinion is delivering the ball according to a man's play, which you must ascertain by strictly watching the movements of the batter; that you will be able to do, by giving him what you would call a good length ball, according to the speed; for instance, Clark 4 and a half yards. Hillyer 5, Wisden 5 and a half. By giving him a few of those to begin with, *as near as you can,* you will be able to find out his particular play, and where he is most deficient. In the present day you will find they are most of them inclined to play back. I should say this has been caused by bowlers not working sufficiently with mind, but always pitching the ball at the same length. When you see this back play, you must force the ball onwards, so as to make the man play out; and the ball is never tossed far enough, till that object is gained; that is, the batsman made to play forward. Perhaps before that is the case, you will have caused him to retire; for instance, in 1850 I drove twelve men on their wickets. If your man is particularly fond of playing back, you must keep repeating the dose; for if he plays out once or twice, he is sure to go back to his old play. If he does not, but tries to hit you forward, he will very likely give a chance, not being used to that style of play. In case he should hit you forward, you will be well prepared for him, by having a man or two placed in the long field. The hit will most likely fetch but one; and if hit up, it may be caught. A short ball is the worst ball a man delivers; the batsman can hit it almost where he chooses, and is likely to give no chances. (There are a few exceptions as to bowlers, whose style won't allow them to over toss the ball, I shall explain this in another part).

A ball over tossed on the contrary makes the batsman play out; and if the ball is not well covered with an upright bat, he is almost sure to give a chance. Therefore, a ball should sooner be over tossed than short. Many bowlers pay no attention to the most essential, and I should say, the prettiest part of the game; that is, the field. I have seen a man deliver the ball, and never look to the field, or see whether they are all there, even before the long stop has got to his place. A bowler must have a high opinion of his own abilities, to think he can beat his opponent without his field.

In laying out your field, you should be careful in selecting good men for your principal places, such as wicket keeper, point, stop, short slip; those posts being well secured, you will be able to move the others at leisure; which you will have to do, if your bowling is pretty correct, which it must be if you are to have an efficient field. How can you lay out a field for an uncertain bowler? How can you tell where the men will hit him? I mean one of the any-how style, happy-go-lucky, yard on this side, yard on the other, all men alike, one straight in about two overs. How careful the Public Schools ought to be in selecting bowlers of a good delivery for their instructors, men who go up to the wicket as if they were going to put the ball somewhere about the mark. On them depends the future style of the learners, who ought not to be taught to throw away all their fine manly strength in empty air. Why, a person who recommends a wild scrambling bowler to teach cricket, ought to be took up under the Cruelty to Animals Act.

A bowler should first try to get a *steady* style of delivery, easy not distressing, and should be sure not to bowl at the very top of his strength, for in that case he must become wild and reckless, losing that precision, which is so necessary to defeat a good batsman. It frequently happens that when a Bowler finds he is dropping the ball short, he will stoop forward and try to propel it with greater force, which will cause him to drop it still shorter and get him into greater difficulties; the very reverse should be the case, when he finds himself that way inclined, he should immediately rear himself as erect as possible, for the more upright a Bowler stands, the greater the ease with which he will deliver the ball, and the more difficult will it be to play: the ball is delivered higher and there is more circle, and the greater the circle the greater the deception to the Batsman. This applies to all sorts of Bowlers. For instance if a Bowler has been forcing a man on his wicket, till he won't submit to it any longer, he may by tossing the ball a little higher and a little shorter so deceive the Batsman that he will play out, though he has been playing balls back that have been pitched a yard farther, and will very likely lose his wicket by this mistake: at the same time he must be careful to deliver with the same action or he will be detected by the Batsman, who will be put on his guard.

The greatest proof that it is not speed alone that tells, but the length according to a man's play, with as much deception as possible, is that you will see a good slow Bowler do as much or more execution on a fine even damp or dead ground than Bowlers of greater speed that have not equal precision. Why is this? But because many Bowlers never study the state of the ground but deliver at the same speed and at the same place, as near as they can, on a dry as on a wet ground. On a dry hard ground five yards would be a good length and difficult to play, but on soft and spongy ground such a ball would be hit away. Therefore it is necessary in such a case to put a little more speed on as well as pitch the ball a little further. This proves my argument that a man should not always bowl with all his strength, but have a little left for particular occasions.

I said it was not speed alone that tells, but I don't wish it to be supposed that I recommend very slow bowling without alteration, a ball must have some pace or a man will walk into it and do as he likes, if he has got legs, though of late years those articles have not been so much exercised as of old, while padding has been substituted for their use.

Nothing tests the truth of Bowling so much as a good level ground, it will find out the bad balls soon enough, and will enable the Batsman to hit them, and perhaps leave so few good ones that the Bowler will be obliged to retire, while on rough ground the same bad balls might have escaped and perhaps even proved effective. Suppose you have what I call a skimming Bowler, for mind you all straight arm Bowlers don't deliver alike. Some sink their body in delivery and turn the elbow in close to the side, which makes the ball more like an underhand one, and causes it to come straight from the hand, so that it is plain, as you can see it all the way, and by placing the bat full at it you will rarely make a mistake. Such a ball has no deception; as it is delivered from the hand so will it rise from the bound. It is no use putting it further up, as there is nothing to deceive the batter, he will drive it forward. This is the part I said I would refer you to. Well such a bowler is seldom any use on level or soft ground. There is no fire in the ball. It won't get up, and being pitched rather short to keep it from being hit forward, can't do any execution. But on a hard uneven or glibby ground such bowling often tells well, but I question if under like circumstances a better style would not tell better.

Though I recommend you to get the style of delivery that is easy to yourself, I don't say that you should be careless or lazy, on the contrary, you must put all your body and mind in a determination to get your man out, and be guarded above all things not to lose your temper. At times it's enough to make you bite your thumbs to see your best balls pulled and sky-rocketed about – all luck – but you must console yourself with, 'Ah, that won't last long.'

Now as for the place for delivering the ball – the bowling crease is three feet on each side the stumps. You will find most men deliver with the foot placed half way betwixt the end of the crease and the wicket, some nearer the wicket. I think this is an error, they ought to deliver at the very end of the crease, for the ball then has to go more across the wicket and is more deceptive to the batter. It is a plan I generally adopt, and if it is advantageous to me that is only half round, how much more it must be to a straight arm bowler.

Now a word as to variation in delivery, such as raising the hand higher and lower. (I am now speaking of Bowling according to the rules.) Variation of speed and height, sometimes higher and sometimes lower, sometimes faster sometimes slower, deceives the batsman. These are all little things, but though appearing trivial may amount to a great deal. But after all that has been said, I have never stated what is the most dangerous ball for a batsman, except the one that gets him out. It is the ball that catches him in two minds, so that he does not know whether to play forward or backward, but plays half way; that's the ball if you can do it. How? By putting the Ball exactly in the right place according to your man's play.

From these hints and observations you must not expect to reap the advantage in a week or a fortnight. Some may profit in years, some never, for –

One science only will one genius fit.
So vast is art, so narrow human wit.

II

On Fielding

In placing the Field the men should be laid out according to the hitting; all batters have favourites hits. When in the Field you should be particular in watching the movements of the batsmen; you should not take your eye off him when in the act of playing, but always expect to have every ball played to you. That will cause you to be on your legs; and, though the ball should be played on the opposite side to where you are, you will get a good start at it, and actually be on your way almost before the batter has played the ball. In returning the ball, you should be sure and try to throw it in breast high. I think the system of making the ball bound before it comes to the wicket is bad. It may shoot, or be turned out of its course, in either case the chance is gone; therefore it is better to throw straight at the man. In nine cases out of ten, it is bad to shy at the wicket. There is the uncertainty of hitting it; and very likely the field will not prepared by backing up; and so you will cause one of those annoying sights, an overthrow. Any fieldsman intentionally shying at the bottom of the wicket, when a man is there to receive the ball, ought to have 'a dozen' immediately. You frequently will see the ball returned hard in, when there is no chance of a run being attempted; this is bad, it affects the wicket keeper's hands, as he is not prepared for it; when there is a chance he would not fell it, if you were to send it in like shot; his anxiety would take away the thought.

You should never hold the ball, but return it to the man at the wicket immediately; if you are in the out field, and the batsman is on the alert, he will steal a run, and you will get laughed at. In throwing in, avoid a long swing of the arm, but shy with as short and sharp a motion as possible.

In catching, you will frequently see the easiest chances missed. For why? Men don't give way sufficiently with their hands. Thinking it easy, they hold their hands stiff, which causes the ball to rebound, and they lose it, with the old saying, 'I made too sure of it.' That's very little consolation to a bowler. Balls hit with the greatest force you will generally see caught; for the man, seeing the ball come with such velocity, feels a little fear, which makes his hands give, and causes the very action that makes the ball stick. Most catches, particularly high or slow ones, are missed for want of humouring the ball.

In gathering to a ball, you should try to get it at the bound, which you will be able to do if well on your legs. At the same time be prepared, in case it should shoot; sometimes it is worth the risk losing a run, by darting in a little further to run the batter out, especially if he is a good one. I think there are no halfway places in the field a man should stand, either to save the one, or the three or four, except in extraordinary cases. The middle off, cover point, long slip, and long stop should all save one run. Those are places that give a man a fine chance of showing off to advantage; for, by being a good judge and a good gatherer, he may frequently run a man out. The distance of those places depends much on the state of the ground. If it is soft, you can stand much nearer than when very hard; because the ball loses half its speed the moment it touches the ground. When you have the office for moving in the long field from the *general*, move a good distance. It is unpleasant to both parties to keep saying 'further yet;' besides, he can sign to you to stop when you have got far enough. This point is difficult to give advice about. It depends on the quality of the bowling. Now, with respect to point, if you have that *any-how* stuff, that you can't tell where it is coming to a yard or so, I should say it is better to fall back, and make yourself useful in the field. However fond a man may be of Cricket, he does not like to stand in a place where he has no chance of defending himself. If the bowling is nearly correct, I am an advocate for standing well up to the batter. There are some whose style of play won't allow them to be dangerous, and to these you may stand very close.

The long stop should place himself at such a distance that he can save the run, and not any nearer. If he could stop the ball close to the wicket, what's the use? He loses the advantage of covering a great space of ground on each side, and saving the tips or touches that frequently occur. The great merit of a long stop is getting to balls that are put a little out of their course, so as to save the run. If you see the batsman trying to get the best of you by stealing a run, gather in a little closer. It is better to prevent him attempting, than to give him the chance of getting it; which he will do, if the ball is not well handled in every way.

If a Batsman has only one good hit, and is weak at all the others, it ought to be very difficult for him to get runs; for if your field is good, and well laid out, and the bowler bowling at points, you can afford to make your field doubly strong in his favourite place. In altering your field, the bowler may have only one more ball to deliver in the over. Some one will be sure to say 'Oh, never mind till next over.' I don't believe in that doctrine. I would have the field altered then and there, as the thing may come off that very ball. Delays are dangerous; and, as a great general said, 'There is a moment to decide a victory.' Though you should have a captain in the field, (as you ought to have, for what is every one's business is never well done), it is proper for him to say to the bowler, 'Don't you think it would be better to do so and so?' It makes it appear as if somebody knew something as well as himself, and there is always a way of speaking to a fielder, so that it will be pleasant for him to receive it, unless it be one of those shake-yourself sort of men that seem to do everything reluctantly; with him you must do as well as you can. These little things all create a good feeling.

I have one more remark: I like to see every man steady at work, I am sure that every one has enough to do when at play in minding his own business, without gossiping or being careless. I used to admire a certain Gentleman, that has left off playing this last two or three years, at the change of the over, walking across the wicket as steady as old Time, and when I was starting to bowl, just glancing round the field to see if they were all ready. There he was sure to be with his eye on every one to see if all was right. There is plenty of time for a little funny saying or something to laugh at, when a man is out, without keeping every one waiting between each over.

III
The Science of Batting
First you should try to get that firm yet easy position that best suits you, so that you may have the freedom of action so requisite for both hitting the bad and the middling balls, and defending your wickets from the good ones, and not be so fixed that you are only prepared to play or hit one or two particular balls. It is the man that hits all round, that is prepared to play the ball on the side it comes that makes the awkward customer for a bowler. Never get too fond of one particular hit. If you do it will lead you into error; I have known it to occur to the very best batters. Sometimes a good leg hitter, sometimes a good off hitter will be getting so partial to his favourite hit, that he will be trying it with straight balls. If bowled out will say for an excuse, 'I thought it was not straight.' A ball straight for the wicket should be played with an upright full faced bat, back towards the bowler, with the handle of the bat inclined forward. There is as much room behind the bowler and often more than in any other part of the field.

There is no halfway play at a good ball: it could be played to the extent of your reach forward, so as to smother it, or back as near as you can safely get to your wicket, by that means there is a longer sight from the bound. Never let the ball get you in two minds, if you do it will cause you to play half way. Ah, there's where all the mischief lies. It is caused by an error in judgment, you are deceived as to the spot on which the ball will pitch, that causes the mistake.

In playing forward take the upper part of your body with you and have the top or left hand placed well on the top side of the handle of your bat and not too far apart from the other hand; by the handle of the bat being nearer the bowling than the blade (always bearing in mind to keep it straight), the ball will be prevented from rising. If you don't take your body with your arms when playing forward, one is undoing what the other is trying to do. Take care not to get a habit of sinking your body when hitting. It takes away your power and not only that but it will cause you to hit under the ball.

Don't stroke with all your strength, a man is often out with hitting at a bad ball. For why? He wants to make too much of it, and by hitting past his strength, loses precision. It is not always the long swinging hit that drives the furthest. No, it is hitting the ball at the proper time, with a quick or short motion of the arms and wrists. If you go out of your ground to hit, you should forget the wicket keeper, if not your mind will be one way your body the other. You must go far enough to cover the ball and drive it straight before you. Never try to pull a straight ball across you. There are many chances against you if you do. For you have only the width of the ball to hit at, while it may chance to rise suddenly or turn out of its course, but if you take your bat upright, straight down the wicket, and play on to the ball, you have the whole length of the bat, always taking care to play the ball with your bat, not the bat with the ball. Lay your bat on to the top of the ball and don't pull your bat from the ground up to it. That is not Cricket. The bat was made to play the ball.

Never make up your mind for a certain ball before it is delivered. Your mind being prepared for one sort of ball and another coming, as is almost sure to be the case, there will most likely be an accident. How often you hear men say, I have not been used to this or that sort of bowling. It's all nonsense, they ought to practice all kinds. If a fast underhand Bowler is put on for a change (what I call a trundling Bowler, who gives a ball that bounds three or four times before it comes to you), he often does execution, specially with the rising generation. Why? – they have only been practising at one style; then they say, the twist of the ball, hop-stride, and jumping before it comes, deceives the eye; they having been used to only one bound and perhaps to one straight ball in the over, and the other being nearly always straight, they are rather alarmed and losing their confidence, the ball goes rolling through the wicket. In reality such balls are the easiest in the world to play. They want no judgment as to playing backwards or forwards. They only want a good full faced bat put to 'em upright with a bit of a drive forward. Play of that kind will beat any Bowler of that style. Though bowling shall be ever so bad, I don't say you shall hit away every ball. No, for it may by chance get up at the proper place, and make itself a good one. But you will be fully prepared by playing in the method I have described. You will see, by what I have said, that it is well to have an hour at 'all sorts', now and then. Besides, it will teach you to be on your legs, and shew you that there are many balls you have been in the habit of merely playing at and laying down, which you might hit away with confidence. For instance, balls over tossed, you will be able to drive forward hard by using your feet, while if you stand screwed to the ground you can only lay them down, and by that means you make a Bowler seem to deliver many more good balls than he really does. There is in short only one true method of play. That is, not to make up your mind till the ball is delivered, then if it be a little too far, play forward; if a little too short, play back. If it be put on the right place be decided, and play either one way, or the other, no halfway.

In running your runs, you should always be prepared to take the advantage; which you will be able to do by leaving your ground as soon as the ball is out of the Bowler's Hand. That will give you the advantage not only by being well on your legs, but by having a less distance to run. But bear in mind not to leave your ground till the ball has quitted the Bowler's hand, or he will be justified in trying to put you out. Nothing looks worse than a man standing like a fixture, perhaps leaning on his bat. Then having to make a start and calling that a hard run, which if he had been prepared he might have walked. Run your first run well in case of any mishap in the field, and be sure always to let your partner know what you are going to do, by shouting at the top of your voice, so that he can't mistake your meaning. How bad it looks to see two men getting into the middle between the wickets and staring at each other, not knowing which way to go for want of decision and speaking out. If a man stands fast to his ground and seems to have no care about the runs, he deadens the play; the Fielders care nothing about him; what puts Fielders about more than when two determined runners get in and take every advantage? I am not an advocate for *overrunning*, for I think men may lose more than they gain by being out of wind, and therefore not so well prepared to play the next ball.

Now you will see some, the harder they hit the more certain they are to run, though the ball be going straight to a man, when if it were hit very slowly they would not attempt it; that speaks badly for their judgment. It should be quite the reverse. The ball hit slowly may be a certain run, while the ball hit with greater force to the same place is not half one; as it gets to the Fielder so much quicker. There are many little advantages to be taken of Fielders, such as the ball going to a man's left or wrong hand, or a man not being able to shy but always jerking in. These points want judgment: they made be done, and often are done by two decided men, who understand each other, but they will not answer with vacillating men. It is never right to risk your innings for the sake of a run. If your innings is only valued at a run, it is not worth much.

IV
On Matchmaking, Managing and Umpiring
When playing a match it is not always right to keep on the same bowling, though the bowlers be bowling ever so well. Suppose you have a fast bowler on, a batsman comes in that don't like slow; or the contrary; why, I say give him what he don't like, never mind persons saying you dare not do this or you dare not do that, if you gain your object by getting the batter out, you may win the match through it. There are plenty of Gentlemen as well as Players, who cannot play both fast and slow. Some would shut their eyes at a fast one, but might perchance swipe away a slow one for four. It's bad judgment to put a fast bowler at a man, who *can't hit*. Why? He may stick his bat down, the ball may hit it and glide away for three or four runs without his having anything to do with it. Such a man with a slow bowler is probably a certainty.

In choosing your side don't choose all batters. In the first place make sure of your bowlers (that's the principal matter), your wicket keeper, your long stop. Then come the batters: five or six there will be no question about. Now as to the one or two last; if you have a middling bat and no fielder; if he gets ten and loses fifteen in the field, he is five worse than nothing : a bad bat and good field saves fifteen in the match, his side have that fifteen less to get; so give me the good field.

Umpiring is a very arduous and often unthankful office, especially in country places, where a jealousy exists on each side, and a doubt of his doing his duty fairly and impartially. That is sure to be the case, when he belongs to one of the parties and is not sufficiently acquainted with the game. It is better to choose men connected with neither party. If you have anything against a man object to him at once, but not on suspicion; with some players Umpires never can be right. Don't let a man take his place and then be dissatisfied with his decisions, and in lieu of making the game a pleasure and creating a good feeling among all, make it quite the reverse. It is difficult for an Umpire to please both parties, but let each give him credit for good intentions. It is impossible for an Umpire to be always right, but I would always take his decision (if he understands the game), before the opinion of a spectator or of one of the players, for he stands in the best position to judge correctly. It is on those nice points, which create a difference of opinion amongst spectators and the field, that the decision of the Umpire is required. How unjust it is to an Umpire. When he has given his best opinion on some nice point (such as the ball grazing a man's bat or glove), for the batsman to go away and say he was not out and so create a bad feeling. I said before there are some (and they ought to know better), who never are out, unless the bowler makes the middle stump turn a summerset.

Umpires have many points to attend to, they have not a moment to lose; and if they allow the eye to wander to any fresh object, that very moment a nice decision may be wanted, so they should let nothing but Cricket and their immediate duty in the game occupy their minds.

In Pitching Wickets I often hear Umpires say 'it'll do', when there is some little object that looks queer at the pitching place. In such case my opinion is it'll not do. The wicket ought to be altered, till it is a good one. I don't like those 'it'll do' wickets. They may either spoil the batting or the bowling, and consequently there may be no play in the match. It is better therefore for both sides, that all objections should be removed if possible, by having as good a wicket as can be got on the ground.

V

Advice to Practice Bowlers

You will often see Practice Bowlers bowl away at all players good and bad alike: that should not be. A Practice Bowler ought to bowl according to the batsman's play. Suppose a Gentleman thinks he should like Cricket, he joins a Club or engages a bowler. Say he has never played; do you think the bowler is justified in knocking down his wicket constantly, or perhaps giving him sundry hits and bruises? No, certainly not. Give him something he can hit to begin with, and that will please him and make him fond of the game, so that he will play again. Then bowl at him according to his improvement. He will so become a player, and perhaps what is of more consequence to cricketing in general, a good supporter of the game. For mind you, it is the Gentleman that makes Cricket by his countenance and support. Besides what's the merit in bowling out a person who has not learned to play? It don't add anything to the reputation of the Bowler. While the gentleman may be made so disgusted that he won't play any more: and so no one left for you to bowl at.

In practice it is often the way to pitch wickets anywhere. That is a bad system. You ought to be particular and have a good wicket, if you mean to have a good practice and be of any service to the person you bowl to. On a good ground he will have confidence and pleasure, all the balls will be playable; on the contrary if the ground is rough, the balls will cut about, he will be hit and lose his confidence and his play. Not half the balls will be playable, so that half the time will be lost. Therefore there ought to be a good wicket. The roller should always be run over the ground at the pitch of the ball before commencing practice, it's well worth ten minutes patience to get good Cricket instead of bad.

I recommend Practice Bowlers to take a little pains with their batting and also to study the science of the game, for they will then be good men to be engaged, even if their bowling is not quite tip top. Clubs it is true when first established usually begin by applying for a first rate bowler. But I think that that is a mistaken notion. Let them begin with a moderate bowler, who is a pretty good bat. The bowling will be quite good enough, while by having one who can bat, they will, by seeing him in now and then, catch the idea and learn to play in a correct method. More can be taught in a week by shewing the manner of play, than by months of talking. Another consideration for Clubs may be that such men are not so expensive.

VI
The Conclusion
Cricket is a noble, manly and athletic game. It adds vigour and health to the whole frame. It is now established so strongly as a national game, that it will never be forgotten. I think I may fairly say that I Zingari and the All-England Eleven have contributed much to establish the good feeling that now exists towards Cricket and Cricketers in all parts of the kingdom, by shewing the science as well as the true spirit of the game, that is by playing with all their skill and determination to beat their opponents and at the same time to be the best of friends with them. Their system allows them to play in all parts of the kingdom more than any other Club, and wherever they have once been I believe they are always welcome again. These matches bring all classes together; men of all shades congregate, folks of all ages meet, if they can't join in the game, they can take a delight in seeing their relations or friends excelling others. The wealthy and great derive advantage from them as well as those inferior in station: they have an opportunity of seeing that there is good sense as well as good dispositions amongst their poorer neighbours, while these gain by mixing in better society an improvement in manners and morals.

Sir, I have gone rather minutely into different parts of the game, to some I may have been tedious, but as I had never read a book where these different points of the game had been sufficiently explained, I determined at your request to try my hand. It's my first attempt and probably the last. If it was making a match or playing it I should be more at home. Take the will then for the deed, and I only hope I shall live to see some who have profited by my remarks. I now conclude, Sir, and hoping that we (I mean you, I and our readers), may all meet in the field in this and future years,

I remain, Sir, Your obedient Servant,
Wm Clark.

Appendix Three
The All-England Eleven Song

This is the song written by William Clarke and often sung at dinners held after the conclusion of matches played by the All-England Eleven. It was published in F.S.Ashley-Cooper's *Nottinghamshire Cricket and Cricketers*, issued in 1923. The song was apparently sung to the tune of 'Rule, Britannia!', the patriotic poem written by James Thompson and set to music by Thomas Arne in 1740.

When cricket first in olden time
Was played by Briton's hardy race,
In that great science they were far behind
The men who now the wickets grace.

Refrain:
Then success to cricket, 'tis a noble game,
It's patronized by Royalty, and men of wealth and fame.

The Marylebone ranks first of all,
It's they who do our Laws control;
And then I Zingari, those trumps with bat and ball,
And the Eleven of All England, composed of great and small.
Then success to cricket, etc.

May honour be its guiding star,
And batsmen well their wickets guard;
Then shall it flourish, shall flourish through the land,
And merit its just reward.
Then success to cricket, etc.

Index

A page number in bold indicates an illustration.